SITTING WITH ELEPHANTS

SITTING WITH ELEPHANTS

LESSONS IN HUMILITY FROM THE AFRICAN BUSH

ENHANCED AND EXPANDED SECOND EDITION

ronald dulek

with illustrations by **abbey ndlovu**

THE UNIVERSITY OF ALABAMA PRESS
TUSCALOOSA

The University of Alabama Press
Tuscaloosa, Alabama 35487–0380
uapress.ua.edu

Typeface: Minion Pro

Cover art: Abbey Ndlovu
Cover design: Sandy Turner Jr.

Cataloging-in-Publication data is available from the Library of Congress.
ISBN: 978-0-8173-6237-9 (Paper)
E-ISBN: 978-0-8173-9585-8 (Ebook)

to Sally,
the best partner one could have had on life's amazing journey

to Dan Dulek and Laura Green,
thanks for letting us grow old in peace and without constraints

to Luella, Timothy, William, and Lucas,
we are humbled and honored to be your grandparents;
by the way, now you know where we were each summer

Contents

Acknowledgments

The following people have provided invaluable support, guidance, and encouragement for this project. John and Mary Burke, the two most eagle-eyed editors I have ever met—and the best friends a family could ask for; Kate Carlson, my favorite daughter-in-law; Valentin Chernikov, my Russian friend, Singaporean associate, and global teaching mentor; Richard Dennelly, a friend, a friendly reader, and a partner from days of old in graduate school; Daniel Dulek, my favorite son; Dell Fisher, a great friend and the only person I know who spent his eightieth birthday visiting our bush house; Carol Gray, a spiritual inspiration and the one person brave enough to visit the bush house in February; Laura Green, my favorite daughter; Robert Green, my favorite son-in-law; Ailsa and Bennie Groenewald, two friends who are jewels hidden in the African bush; Benton Gup, a friend and colleague; Nancy Hauter, an OSHA colleague, long-time friend, and world-class travel companion; Joe Hornsby, the smartest person in the YMCA weight room; Jan Jones, a true friend who believes in me in spite of my faults; Marte Knopick, my favorite cousin and constant inspiration; Johan Lawson, my bush teacher, friend, and spiritual example; Mark and Tiffany McLean, our first visitors in Africa; Jackie and Milton Mayfield, former doctoral students who are now my teachers; Jef Naido, a colleague, friend, coauthor, travel companion, and native South African; Katie Nakagaki, my second cousin, friend, and insightful world traveler; Lou Marino, my adopted brother, fantastic friend, and long-time teaching partner; Barry Mason, a leader's leader; Joyce Meyer, a colleague and friend who strives for excellence daily; Mary Piland, an inspiring friend and world-class conversationalist; Dick and Lynn Slattery, the definition of sophistication; Judy Spadoni, proof that a life of service can give happiness; Ron Springer, the world's greatest neighbor and a fan of Africa; Linda Spurling, a long-time friend and OSHA colleague; Mike and Jamie

Stanley, bridge friends and our most recent visitors; Lonnie Strickland, my best friend for forty-eight years; Mary Stone, a person of brilliance; Tom and Lisa Thayer, a couple that proves business people can have fun; Daniel Waterman, an early advocate, wonderful advisor, and mentor without peer throughout this book's creation; Marilyn Whitman, an inspiration to all and a teacher par excellence; and Eric Williams, a friend, colleague, and advocate for what is right.

Anything good in this book is due to the advice of these friends. All faults are owed to my own incompetence.

Introduction: Squeeze the Juice

Do not go gentle into that good night,
Old age should burn and rave at close of day;
Rage, rage against the dying of the light.
—Dylan Thomas

It ain't the heat. It's the humility.
—Yogi Berra

Most people who visit Africa capture the experience through photos. I do it through words. Fortunately, this edition of *Sitting with Elephants* will use both words and drawings to share the experience of our African adventures. The words come through electronic messages sent to our adult children, Dan Dulek and Laura Green. The drawings come through illustrations provided by Abbey Ndlovu, a highly talented African artist with whom I've been friends for over a decade. Abbey works full time as a guard at Sabie Park, the compound in which our house is located. His drawings display a level of talent that, in my opinion, deserves a wider audience. Abbey has, as you will see throughout this book, an amazing ability to capture the feeling and the spirit of the African bush. Hopefully, my words and Abbey's illustrations will combine to share not just the story of our African summer adventures but also the emotion, the excitement, and the awe of the Africa bush. It is truly an amazing, sacred place.

The story begins in 2007 when Sally, my wife, and I decided to buy a house in South Africa. I was one week away from being fifty-seven years old; Sally was three weeks away from being fifty-eight. Our life in the United States was disturbingly comfortable. At the time Sally was a librarian at a local elementary school; I was, and still am, a business professor at the University of Alabama. Our children were grown, had moved out, and were functioning independently.

Every semester I would lecture undergraduate, graduate, and executive business students about the need to "Squeeze the Juice." "Don't spend your entire career in a cubicle," I proclaimed passionately. "Take some chances, go out and do things, live life!" At the conclusion of these lectures, I returned to my office, caught up on emails, read a paper or two, and trudged home at 5:30 to eat, watch television, and go to sleep.

One night I shared with Sally my fear of living a hypocritical life. This discussion led to an examination of various alternatives. We realized that with a little planning and some financial belt-tightening, we could free up our summers. That freedom meant we could live wherever we desired. We therefore asked ourselves, "What if we bought a bush house in South Africa?" It seemed more exciting than buying a condominium in Florida. We were not raging against getting old, yet we recognized the tick-tock of time. Our remaining minutes were going to be spent no matter what we did. So we decided to spend them differently. We chose to "Squeeze the Juice" by aligning ourselves with Nike's "Just Do It!" rather than Del Webb's "Live on." We have since spent the past eighteen summers living in the African bush.

The continent to which we were moving was not totally foreign to us. We are not that naïve. We had spent a few weeks in Africa each of the previous three years. Two of those visits were to South Africa; one was to Kenya and Tanzania. Our favorite part of each of those visits was the time we spent in the bush. So we knew that we enjoyed the location. Plus, the summer before making the purchase, we rented a bush house in an area called Marloth Park, a community that borders the southern side of Kruger National Park, the largest game reserve in Africa. That Marloth Park test adventure, though at times a bit frightening, proved enjoyable.

Yet the story gets stranger. We bought the bush house over the internet . . . sight unseen. We found pictures of the house on a website and learned that it is in a nature preserve called Sabie Park. We had never been to that specific location, but we were familiar with the general area. We knew that Sabie Park and the house bordered the western edge of Kruger National Park. An examination of local maps showed the house was close to one of the park entrances—the Paul Kruger Gate. We had visited Kruger National Park on those other trips to South Africa and knew that Skukuza, the park's headquarters, was twelve kilometers from the Paul Kruger Gate.

Two friends, Lonnie Strickland, a colleague at the University of Alabama and the person who introduced us to South Africa and the African bush, and Mike Crosbie, a South African who taught at UNISA, the University of South Africa, happened to be in the area at the time. We asked them to look at the house with the listing realtor. Unfortunately, or perhaps by design, the realtor brought the wrong keys and could not open the door; as a result, Lonnie and Mike looked through the windows but never entered the house. They verified that a house existed. They also explored Sabie Park and reported it was beautiful. That was enough for us. We made an offer.

We tried to get the realtor and the homeowner to wait ten months to complete the purchase. That was the earliest that we could return to Africa. But, understandably, neither wanted to take the house off the market for that long. So, in the end, we negotiated the following deal with the realtor: we will purchase the house sight unseen; then, if we do not like the house when we come to live in it next June, you will resell it without taking a commission. Not a great deal, but it was the best we could do. So we bought a house in the African bush without ever seeing it, walking inside of it, or even visiting the area in which it was located. How is that for "Squeezing the Juice"?

But the house is just a part of the story. The true centerpiece of our African adventure involves a herd of wild African elephants that comes to the fence in our backyard. To say we are friends is presumptuous. To say that we have become acquainted and want to learn more about each other is definitely on target.

Weighing in at an average of five tons, these elephants intimidate even the most courageous. But intimidation turns to admiration as you watch and get to know elephants. Their intellect, their capacity for empathy, their ability to love lead you to the realization that elephants have characteristics equal, if not superior, to humans. They are magnificent beings.

At its heart, then, this book is an adventure story about living in the African bush, a tale about a relationship with a herd of elephants and a love story about Africa. Sally and I dearly love Africa—or at least our little part of it. We care deeply about the setting, the wildlife, and the people. We consider many of the people our friends, in the best sense of the word. Some of the best parts of this book explore these African relationships, their meaning, and their significance.

Of course, like all romances, this relationship has highs and lows. Seeing leopards in the driveway, lions in the front yard, and herds of elephants at the back fence qualify as highs. One never gets bored with these events. Witnessing endemic poverty, hungry people remove and eat food from dirty trash cans, poaching, and senseless violence—these are the lows. Challenges such as these prevent a place from ever becoming ideal.

In the end, though, we have come to realize that it is easy to love a place or a person that is perfect. It's more challenging to acknowledge another's flaws and still love that place or person. It is this latter type of love that we feel for our corner of Africa. We love it in spite of its flaws.

But beyond the adventure, the elephants, and the love story, this book has one more facet to it: this book is a reflection about what we have learned through our African forays. It is a waste of money and effort to go to Africa, Antarctica, Asia, or even the local Walmart merely for the adventure. One should reflect on and learn from the experience as well. To paraphrase Socrates, the unexamined adventure is not worth having.

At the outset, let me share the single most important lesson that has emerged from our African interactions: an appreciation for humility. Any non-native who engages with Africa, its people, and its wildlife and fails to become more humble has missed the important lesson that Africa continuously teaches. Anyone who reads this book and fails to examine his or her life from a humbler perspective has missed a significant part of this book's message as well.

We freely admit that the virtue of humility seems out-of-date in a world that covets self-promotion. It is difficult to see the benefit of humility in a society dominated by selfies, TikTok, Tumblr, and X. Even more, it is difficult to argue for the value of humility in a world that measures worth in "likes" and "followers." Even the word "influencer" has taken on broader meaning thanks to its use in social media.

So a humble perspective is worth considering. Buddha, Jesus, Muhammad—each encouraged humble servitude over self-promotion. Mahatma Gandhi, Nelson Mandela, Mother Teresa—each proved that it works. We personally guarantee that if you want to sit with a herd of elephants, humility is essential.

Briefly defined, humility is the recognition that you are not the center of the universe. Humility involves having a modest view of our accomplishments, rank, opinions, and beliefs. The humble even acknowledge that they may sometimes be mistaken. This recognition of one's fallibility encourages humble people to be courteously respectful of others' opinions and beliefs. Humble people listen. More importantly, they listen not to contradict or disprove but to better understand the insights of others. The humble regard others as teachers from whom they can learn, not students to whom they must lecture. These qualities are, by the way, the essence of great leadership.

Finally, humble people are comfortable in their condition. They have no need to be the center of attention. The humble can lead when necessary, but they can follow and support as well. Stated simply, the humble readily acknowledge that other people and other purposes are often more important.

To experience Africa is to experience humility. To stand on the edge of a lake and hear the lonely, beautiful cry of an African fish eagle; to watch a giraffe stretching its neck to capture the top leaves from an acacia tree; to witness a cackle of hyena pups playing joyfully in an open field; to watch a pack of wild dogs yelp, jump, and scamper back and forth while trotting along an old dirt path; to sit with a herd of elephants—each is a lesson in humility. Our talents and accomplishments pale in comparison.

So this book is simultaneously an African adventure story, a tale about elephants, a story about love, and a series of lessons about becoming humbler. The medium for conveying these diverse messages is a series of emails sent to our adult children, supported by beautiful illustrations. We initially wrote the emails to record and share our African experiences with our children. Over time we realized that others might be interested in these stories as well. We hope you find the adventures entertaining, the elephants enchanting, the love affair empowering, the reflections thought-provoking, and the illustrations engaging. And we invite you to pause as you read along and reflect on how you might live and see your life differently if you humbly seek to "Squeeze the Juice."

SITTING WITH ELEPHANTS

CHAPTER ONE

Elephant Ping-Pong

For some reason, Ping-Pong came very natural to me.
—Forrest Gump

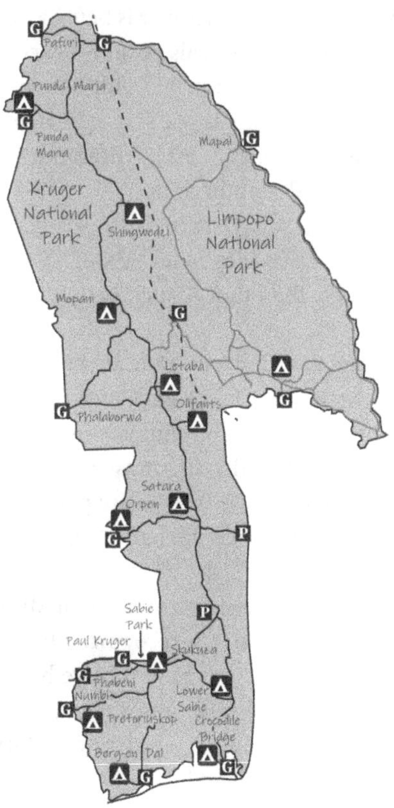

Kruger National Park is not humble. Established in 1898 to protect the wildlife of the Lowveld, the park has evolved into a massive size just short of two million hectares. The park is slightly smaller than Rwanda but larger than Eswatini, formerly known as the Kingdom of Swaziland. From the perspective of the United States, the park's area is equal in area to the state of Massachusetts. Kruger is frequently called the Crown Jewel of Africa.

Kruger National Park—or, as the locals call it, "the Kruger"—contains approximately 2,000 plants, of which 404 are woody plants and 224 are grasses. It also has 53 varieties of fish, 34 amphibian species, 118 different kinds of reptiles, 517 types of birds, and 147 different kinds of mammals. Thousands of animals reside in the area, including bird species such as vultures, eagles, and storks. And, of course, roaming throughout the park are members of the Big Five: lions, leopards, rhinos, buffaloes, and elephants.

What is humbling about the Kruger is being a visitor. Stated simply, visitors are caged while the animals go free. Fences around the camps encircle the visitors, not the animals. With only a few exceptions, the Kruger's guests must remain in cars or game drive vehicles unless they are inside one of the eight enclosed camps. Animals roam freely throughout the remainder of the area.

Elephants have long been a mainstay of Kruger National Park. The park contains over 14,500 elephants. About 15 percent of these elephants are lone bulls; the other 85 percent are members of breeding herds.

The Letaba Elephant Hall museum at the Letaba Rest Camp exemplifies the park's interest in its elephants. Here, visitors can learn about the breeding patterns, communication techniques, and family lives of elephants. Additionally, the museum offers pictures and replicas of Kruger's tuskers. These tuskers are past and present elephants living within Kruger who have the largest tusks. It is a most impressive display.

We visited Letaba and the elephant museum during one of our first forays into the Kruger. The area is recognized for the large number of elephants residing nearby. It was here that we had our first major encounter with elephants. This encounter taught us much, both about the playfulness and about the dangers of wild African elephants. At times these traits go hand in hand.

Dear Dan and Laura,

We are spending two nights in Letaba, a Kruger camp six hours north of Sabie Park. We wanted to see a different part of Kruger and thought that this area might be worth exploring. It has proven more exciting than we anticipated.

Kruger camps close at 5:30 p.m. during this time of year. People go for game drives right before then, because many animals become active late in the afternoon and in the early evening. We, of course, are right there to witness the action.

Kruger personnel strictly enforce that 5:30 closure time. Steep fines are imposed on those who enter the camp after the gates close. The fines are not just a fundraising mechanism; getting people into the camps before dark is imperative to safety. The risk to visitors is significantly greater after dark since the animals are more mobile; the risk to animals is also greater since a driver's vision is not as acute.

So it was 5:00 p.m., and we were driving on the dirt roads surrounding the Letaba camp. No other cars were in the area. We spotted two southern ground hornbills nearby and spent ten minutes watching them. These birds have bright red heads and distinct white markings on their body, but their overall cast is black. They look like the mating outcome of a turkey and a vulture. Fascinating, but not attractive.

After the southern ground hornbills disappeared into the bush, we checked the time and agreed that we needed to scoot back to camp. We were ten minutes away, but we needed that extra time to stop and watch in the event that we saw something else.

We passed a small group of elephants as we headed toward Letaba. The group was fifty meters off the road. One of these elephants was huge; he was easily four meters tall. We slowed to look at him but didn't stop because of the camp time deadline.

Then, about one hundred meters beyond this first group of elephants, we saw a second set. These elephants were closer to the road, with some standing right beside it. Another massively large elephant was in this group. I'm avoiding the word "herd" here because I suspect it was all one herd that had temporarily split apart to devour different chunks of Kruger.

We slowed to a crawl as we drove toward this group. The elephants were close, and we were concerned about possibly hitting one if it meandered onto the road. As we got to within five meters of the group, one of the elephants, the huge one, walked onto the road. He then turned toward our car and started coming toward us. He was waving his ears, raising his trunk, and trumpeting loudly.

Discretion being the better part of valor, I backed the car up. That stopped the charge. The elephant turned back and resumed eating from a tree close to the road.

Then things got complicated. We waited for the elephant to move, but he seemed content standing on the road. Eventually, because of time pressures, I started to move the car toward him. That moment elicited the same reaction as before: the elephant charged toward us waving his ears, swinging his trunk, and trumpeting loudly. We tried a third time as well and then concluded he was not going to let us through.

Fortunately, we had a map and were able to determine that we could turn around and take a different set of roads back to Letaba. However, the distance was about twenty-five kilometers, which meant we would not get back by 5:30. Seeing no alternative, we looked in a guidebook and found a phone number for the Letaba camp. Mom called the camp to explain the circumstances as I began the process of turning the car around on the narrow dirt road.

The elephant watched with apparent glee as we turned the car around. He seemed to think he had achieved his purpose. But then, just as we completed the turn and got ready to give it some gas, Mom shouted, "Oh my God." I looked forward and discovered that the large elephant from the group we had passed earlier was now standing in the middle of the road, ten meters from us.

I froze. This elephant was too close for us to move forward. He was facing us directly. His trunk was hanging straight down—almost to the dirt. His ears were pressed beside his head. His tusks were aimed directly at the car. Unlike the other elephant, this one was silent.

We were trapped between two behemoths! Mom was frightened—okay, full confession, so was I. Her response was action-oriented: "Do something!" My response was philosophical: "Do what?"

This second elephant stood still in the road and seemed to study our situation. He seemed to understand and enjoy the "trap" we were in. I backed the car up slowly, just a meter or two, to get some room between us. I was aware that the other elephant was behind us. I had no desire to irritate him.

After about five minutes, the second elephant, the one in whose direction the car was still facing, stepped off the road. He seemed to be inviting us to pass. But then, as I moved the car forward, he stepped onto the road to block us. When he did this, I again stopped and backed up. We repeated this process twice—with the elephants moving into the road each time the car came forward. Stated simply, we were playing cat and mouse with elephants.

I looked back to see what had happened to the other huge elephant. He left the tree he was chewing and moved further off to the side of the road. I backed up about two meters and turned the car around, again. We then started heading forward. But the moment we did, the first elephant came charging back onto the road. He was again flapping his ears, raising his trunk, and trumpeting in an aggressive manner that said, "You want a piece of this action? Bring it on!"

So to put a few more kilometers on the car—read that ironically since we weren't going anywhere—I turned the car around again. We were now again facing the second elephant.

We paused to discuss the situation as rationally as possible. This second elephant seemed calmer. He wasn't raising his trunk, flapping his ears, and trumpeting like a maniac. He was just moving on and off the road. We thus agreed that this direction was our best avenue for escape. I did, I must confess, continue checking the rear and side-view mirrors for the other elephant as we assessed the situation. He had returned to munching on the tree beside the road and was occasionally glancing at us. I thought he was laughing at our situation.

Our initial calls to the Letaba camp were unsuccessful, but we kept trying. Eventually, someone answered and listened to our dilemma. The Letaba official told us that he would make a note about our late arrival. He then added that we should "be careful."

"Thanks," I responded. I then asked, "Could you explain *how* to be careful?" But the official had hung up the phone.

We played cat and mouse with this second elephant three more times. To complicate matters further, the sun had set, so our vision was limited to the area lit by the car's headlights. We therefore couldn't see the elephant clearly until it walked onto the road. Most of the time we could only guess where it was until it was standing directly in front of us.

By now we had pretty much given up trying to determine the location of the elephant behind us. It was too dark to see. If that elephant wanted to come, sit on the car, and crush us, there was nothing we could do about it. We probably would not know what he was doing until he sat down.

Finally, after about fifteen minutes, I started to move the car toward the second elephant again. This time he didn't step into the road. Then, just as we got to where he had previously entered the road, we heard a loud trumpeting that sent shivers through both of us. The elephant, at this point, was perpendicular to the car and was charging toward it. We could see his outline in the moonlight and could hear him crushing the bush as he came forward. I stomped on the gas and could feel the gravel hitting the back of the car. I assumed other pieces of gravel were flying behind us. If the other elephant were in back of us, he was getting stoned. But we escaped unharmed, although rattled to the bones.

We arrived at Letaba at 7:36 p.m. I thought we would have to pay a fine, but the gate guard let us enter without punishment. He had already heard of our dilemma. The guard's observation, which seemed a bit casual since he had not been involved in the incident, was, "Don't take it too seriously. Those elephants were just playing with you."

"Yes," I thought, "that was a fun game of elephant Ping-Pong. The only problem was that we were the Ping-Pong balls."

But since he didn't fine us, I simply replied, "Thanks. I'm sure you're right."

I hope you folks are well.

Love,
Dad, the Elephants' Ping-Pong Ball

As we learned more about elephants over the intervening years, we discovered that the escape route we selected was not the most advisable. Elephants who are not serious about their intent—those that may be playing with you or just want you to move—do a mock charge. This mock charge involves loud trumpeting, flapping ears, and a raised trunk. Elephants who are intent on harm roll up the trunk for protection or leave it hanging loosely toward the ground. These elephants lay their ears flat against their heads and point their tusks directly at the object to be attacked. This charge is usually silent. Thus, the elephant we chose to pass was the more dangerous.

Sometimes, as the adage goes, it is "better to be lucky than good." In this instance, we were lucky. But we realized that luck can run out. We knew that the next time we might not be so fortunate. In short, we decided that if we wanted to live beside elephants in the bush, then it was time to begin learning about them.

CHAPTER TWO

Guidelines for Approaching an Elephant

I often wondered whether any of the others grasped that I had done it solely to avoid looking a fool.
—George Orwell "Shooting an Elephant"

Being close to a wild African elephant is mesmerizing. The average size of a grown bull elephant is 5.5 tons, with some growing up to 8 tons. That average weight is 1.21 times the weight of a hippopotamus. The weight of a full-size elephant is slightly more than the estimated weight of a Tyrannosaurus rex. The average female elephant comes in at a "slimmed down" 3.25 tons—slightly more than four full-size pickup trucks. Bulls stand over 10 feet tall; females come in between 8 to 9 feet high. The trunks contain more than 4,000 muscles. For comparison purposes, a human body contains 640 muscles. These trunk muscles are put to good use, since the trunk assists in duties such as smelling, sensing, eating, and drinking.

But no anatomical description does justice to an elephant. It is when you are up close and personal that you truly recognize the magnificence of the animal. If you are fortunate enough to get that view in the elephant's natural bush environment, then you will be all the more fascinated. In the bush, you witness the elephant's strength as it pulls down trees with its trunk, almost without effort. In the bush, you see the ballerina-like delicacy in the elephant's feet as it walks gently and softly across the roughest of terrains. In the bush, you stare with astonishment as the elephant seems to randomly dig into a dry riverbed and then suddenly unearths a spring of freshwater. Being close to and observing a wild African elephant is truly a humbling experience.

The backyard of our bush house borders Kruger National Park. A thin wire fence separates the house from the park. The purpose of the fence is to keep out lions and elephants. Even though the backyard is filled with trees, weeds, and thorny bushes, it is still navigable. We meander through the scrub to a pleasant dirt path that parallels the wire fence. Walking beside this fence is particularly enjoyable since it is immediately beside the Kruger; only now, we are not encased in a cage or in a car. We are in the open: free and unrestricted, yet vulnerable. It is a bit risky, but it is a risk worth taking.

One reason to take this risk is that we sometimes see herds of elephants walking along distant hills in the Kruger. These rolling hills form the banks of the Sabie River. Elephants enjoy walking along this terrain.

A grove of trees behind our bush house provides heavy shade to the area. The trees extend from the yard into the Kruger. We were at first a bit disappointed by the presence of these trees since they restrict our view into the Kruger. Over time, though, we learned the benefit of these trees: they provide a safe place for elephants to congregate. And it is there that our elephant education began.

Dear Dan and Laura,

Just a quick note to share yesterday's major event. Our South African friends from Centurion, Mike and Lynda Crosbie, are visiting. We took a six-hour drive in the Kruger and saw two rhinos, lots of impala, a sounder of warthogs, scores of zebra, quite a few giraffes, and lots of elephants, the latter of which were all far away. As we wound our way down the driveway to the house, we agreed that, all in all, it had been a good day of animal viewing. But there was more to come.

I parked in the carport and helped Mike get out of the car and into the house. Recall that Mike's physical condition is such that he is fully confined to a wheelchair. But he is amazingly mobile with the chair. And since our house is flat, he can move around with ease.

Once Mike was situated in the house, I returned to the carport and began removing empty water bottles and other paraphernalia from the car. It was about 5:00 p.m., and there was still ample light outside. Some noises came from the back of the house, and I assumed that Lynda and Mom had wandered onto the back stoep, the veranda that's at the back of the house.

As I listened carefully to the noises, I realized that the sounds indicated that branches and reeds were being broken in half. I doubted that Lynda and Mom were doing that, so I walked along the side of the house to see what was happening. As soon as I cleared the side of the house, I saw the source of the noise: a full herd of elephants—fifteen in all—was ambling about on the Kruger side of the fence. And when I say "side," I mean "beside"! Many were centimeters away from the fence. How ironic. We had been driving for six hours, trying to see elephants up close, and here they were in our backyard.

I went into the house and got Mike, Lynda, and Mom to come onto the back stoep to watch. A couple of elephants noticed us but seemed unperturbed. If anything, their look kind of said, "Yes, we're here. There is no need for either of us to make a fuss. We won't hurt you so long as you don't bother us."

The herd was obviously a family. There were three babies—each of which came up in height to the bottom of their mothers' stomachs. Mike said that means they were about a year old. Others were adolescents and some were young adults. And, of course, there were ample massive ones, one of whom seemed fully in charge. The leader, Lynda said, is called the matriarch. When she chose to leave—the matriarch, not Lynda—everyone else followed.

The elephants ambled off toward the Sabie River as dusk settled over the area. But they left their mark on the area. This morning I noticed five branches from nearby trees have been broken off, stripped of their leaves, and thrown heedlessly on the ground. Additionally, a number of reeds had been pulled up, munched on, and tossed aside. All in all, it looks like a Sunday buffet assaulted by a busload of patrons who ate and left rapidly.

I hope you folks are well.

Love,
Dad, the Elephant Observer

This appearance of the elephants in the backyard was the first of what would be more than one hundred visits over the next eighteen years. The elephants sometimes come to eat the reeds, but more often they come for the shade and to rest in the protection provided by the trees. A place to eat and rest, not a bad combination.

Some winters multiple herds visit; other winters, the same herd visits—or at least parts of the same herd visit—multiple times. Often, herds bring their entire family to the fence, including babies who tend to plunk onto the ground for a quick nap. These rest periods are interesting to observe since the senior elephants form a protective circle around the babies as soon as they fall asleep. In other instances, lone elephants come to the fence to eat and find shady relief from the midday sun. But each visit is similar in one way: it delivers extreme excitement. One never tires of having elephants in the backyard.

A tendency we noticed during the first visit from the elephants, and one that lasted for many years thereafter, is the manner in which the elephants respect the thin wire fence that separates the Kruger from Sabie Park. The initial fence was dilapidated and desperately in need of repair. It has since been upgraded. The initial fence was supposedly electrified, but Sabie Park personnel confirmed that the electricity worked sporadically at best. No matter. For years the elephants recognized the importance of having a barrier to separate us. They never challenged the fence. In fact, the elephants walked beside the fence so frequently that they created a path on the Kruger side of the fence. The fence therefore straddles two paths. The path on the Sabie Park side of the fence is for humans to follow; the path on the Kruger side of the fence is for elephants and other animals to use. We should also add that we have never seen an elephant make a misstep and accidentally bump into the fence. Despite their size, elephants are sure-footed.

Human nature being what it is, we inevitably want more—a little more excitement, a little faster pace. If the fruit is not giving enough juice, you need to squeeze it tighter. This tendency, which happens even with elephants visiting your backyard, resulted in a desire to make the elephant visits more intriguing, more exciting, more on the edge. Stated simply, I wanted to get closer to the herd.

Initially, we watched the elephants from the back stoep of our bush house. There, to one side, we have a plunge pool for protection. A plunge pool is a large outdoor concrete bathtub used to cool off during the hot summer months. On the other side, we have a large brick wall that extends outward from the house to form the back stoep. Behind these two structures is a large sliding-glass door that we can scoot behind if things become dangerous. It seems safe, perhaps too safe. It's difficult to "Squeeze the Juice" while sitting at a table and observing.

So as time passed and the herd visits became more common, I began to move off the stoep and edge a meter or two closer to the fence. The plunge pool and the house were still nearby, but there was an element of excitement to moving slightly beyond their protective custody. Eventually, wandering even a couple of meters away from the house seemed inadequate. I wanted to get closer. I was, however, unsure about the safety of such a venture. So before choosing to do so, I decided to seek expert advice on the matter. This need for expert advice brings us to the Protea Hotel at Kruger Gate.

The Protea Hotel at Kruger Gate, which we will hereafter refer to as the Protea, is a subsidiary of Marriott. This subsidiary, which is called the Protea Hotel Group, operates more than one hundred hotels throughout eight African countries. A distinguishing feature of the Protea group is that each hotel has a distinctive flavor that reflects its local setting. The Protea Hotels in Cape Town and Johannesburg are cosmopolitan and trendy. The promotional literature calls these "Fire and Ice." The Protea Hotel beside Johannesburg's O.R. Tambo International Airport has an industrial motif; it resembles an aircraft hangar with airplane wings, engines, and other equipment scattered throughout. This theme reflects the area's industrial roots and its location as a transportation hub.

The Protea Hotel at Kruger Gate has an African bush theme. Dark, wooden planks form the entrance to the hotel. The front desk has a roof but is actually outside; most of the surrounding parts are open and natural. A heavily wooded forest with a small water pond sits in the middle of the complex. Monkeys frequent the area. Two restaurants in the back have outside dining under a beautiful veranda. It's all very African.

The Protea at Kruger Gate plays an important part in this African adventure story. First, it is the only nearby place to eat. The hotel is located directly across the highway from Sabie Park. Whenever we are tired of our home cooking, we head to the Protea for bush versions of breakfast, lunch, or dinner.

A second reason the Protea is important is that the hotel has an enclosed library/lounge sitting area, as well as a small television room. The library/lounge has a fireplace and comfortable couches. The television room is smaller but has two couches and an internal space heater. Both of these rooms make living in the African bush more tolerable. Although we have never spent the night at the Protea, we have often retreated to the confines of the lounge and the television room on cold winter evenings when the temperature approaches 0 degrees Celsius. It's one thing to sleep bundled up in the cold; it's an entirely different story to sit in a jacket in a cold house, waiting to go to sleep. The Protea provides a much-needed refuge when winter cold prevails.

The Protea was also the site of one of the most invigorating, fun, hopeful, and humbling evenings we have ever had. This event occurred in 2010 while South Africa was hosting the World Cup. The experience provided a moment of hope not just for South Africa but for the world.

Dear Dan and Laura,

Just a quick note to share a really cool international incident. If I were asked to title this email, it would be: "The Way the World Should Be."

We had dinner at the Protea Hotel this evening and then stayed to watch a World Cup soccer match. Ghana was playing Paraguay. Almost everyone in the hotel—and perhaps on the continent—is cheering for Ghana. It is the last remaining African team in the World Cup.

We had dinner in our usual spot at the Protea—in the library beside the fireplace—and then proceeded to the television room to get ready for the game. We were early, so we the first to settle into the room. Our hope was that we would have the room to ourselves, but that desire was a bit naïve during a major World Cup game.

A few minutes after we made ourselves comfortable, a middle-aged, white South African couple joined us. They were followed by a Muslim family of five. This latter group consisted of two males with appropriate Middle Eastern garb, a female in full regalia, including a hijab—only her eyes were showing—and two children. The children were eight to ten years old and dressed in Western fashion.

The room has only two couches, so it was getting a little crowded. We shared a couch with the South African couple, while the Muslim couple sat alone on the other couch. Their children were on the floor. The Muslim woman and I were positioned at the adjoining ends of our respective couches. We were no more than half a meter apart.

Immediately before the game began, the hotel manager opened the door and announced that a number of staff children were going to watch the game with us. Eight African children immediately entered and took over what little floor space was left. The room was packed. The children ranged in age from eight to twelve years old. They were well-behaved, but like children around the world, there was a lot of pushing, shoving, laughing, and teasing. Overall, it was a diverse and enjoyable group.

All matters of physical inconvenience disappeared the moment the game began. I confess that I have become fascinated by soccer. Most of the time it is tediously boring—at least in retrospect—yet at the time one can easily get pulled in by the crowd. When that ball gets close to the net, everyone starts cheering and anticipating something good happening.

Ghana had lots of shots close to the net early in the game but failed to score. Everyone in the room cheered, and we were all having a good time, even though the score was "nil-nil." To paraphrase *Cool Hand Luke*, sometimes nothing can be a pretty interesting game. Incidentally, "nil-nil" is a soccer term. No matter, the children and the adults were having a fantastic time cheering wildly every time Ghana came close to scoring.

The excitement of the game erased racial and ethnic lines. The Black children began giving the Muslim children high fives whenever a player came close to scoring. The Muslim children began giving high fives to their mom and dad as well as the other male present. Then, the next thing you know, Mom and I are giving high fives to the South Africans and to the Black and Muslim children. We were all just having a grand high-five time. It was the way the world should be.

But wait . . . it wasn't over yet. The game continued as a nil-nil thriller. The tension and excitement continued to mount. It's difficult to comprehend how "nothing" can be so exciting, but it was. Then, suddenly, Ghana cane really close to scoring, and a player for Paraguay blocked the shot by going into the net. He broke the rules to block the shot, and the game had to stop while the officials determined how to punish the player. Lots of shouting in many different languages engulfed the room. People in Johannesburg could probably hear us. Even though I know nothing about soccer,

I was shouting as well. I mean, what the hell? As they used to say in Brooklyn, "We was robbed."

The final ruling was that Ghana got a free kick on the goal. That satisfied the people in our television room, so another series of high fives went around.

But this time, in the middle of the excitement, something weird happened. The hijab-clad Muslim woman sitting beside me turned and offered me her hand for a high five. I looked, prepared to raise my hand, and then realized that I wasn't at all sure it was an appropriate cultural move. Could I touch her? If I did, would others consider her violated? Even more importantly, if I touched her, would I be accused of violating her?

So I raised my hand but then paused. I looked first at the woman's face and noticed a pair of sparkling eyes behind all of that cloth. The eyes seemed to say, "Go ahead, let's live for once." But I wanted more than permission from her. *She isn't the one who would kill me*, I thought to myself half lightheartedly and half seriously. For while she may have wanted to live it up, I just wanted to live.

Strangely, at that moment I also had a very humbling recognition of my own biases. My cultural ignorance might be excusable since I had never before confronted this kind of situation. But my fears and concerns, especially my thought about being killed if I responded inappropriately, demonstrated Western biases to a Middle Eastern situation. Up to that point everyone in the room had been affable and friendly. Yet now I was worried about being killed? I quickly realized that this response, even if it is meant in humorous exaggeration, was neither funny nor appropriate. *You should be better than this*, I told myself.

Fortunately, the woman's husband noticed what was happening and took control of the situation. Our gazes locked for what seemed like a minute but was probably only five seconds. His eyes were not sparkling, but they were not angry either. If anything, his gaze indicated appreciation for my hesitancy.

So he waited a moment longer, perhaps to relish his authority in this situation, and then in a very deep, official voice proclaimed, "You may touch my wife." So I slapped a high five on her, and the room erupted with additional cheers. Even Mom was smiling and laughing. I then stood up, walked over to the husband, and gave him a high five as well. He grinned broadly to signal his appreciation of the gesture.

The score at the end of the game—and after an added time for a playoff—was still nil-nil. A shoot-out followed, with Paraguay ultimately winning the match.

Everyone left at the same time. We were disappointed by the loss, exhausted from our efforts, but bonded in a manner that none of us ever expected. All of us felt exhilarated by what we had experienced together. Each knew that it had been a very special night. For a brief, shining moment, we had gotten to experience the way the world should be.

I hope you folks are well.

Love,
Dad, the High-Fiving Diplomat

When we first moved to Sabie Park, the internet connection in the preserve was unreliable. Dropped signals and failed connections were common. Desperate for a better connection, I visited the hotel manager at the Protea and asked for help. For the first year or two, he charged us a fee to connect to the hotel's internal system. Later, as the manager noticed the amount of time and money we spent at the Protea, he allowed us to connect for free. The agreed upon place for the connection is the television room.

With this agreement in place, our life in the bush began to follow a consistent pattern. In a nutshell, I would rise early each morning, drive to the Protea, buy a pot of coffee, and spend an hour or two in the television room, using the internet. Few hotel guests use the television room at this time; however, various grizzled safari guides hang out there between jobs. This shared space led to some interesting conversations. An aging American professor who hangs around in the television room piqued the interest of these hardened African safari guides. They wanted to know why I was in Africa, what I was doing here, and what my life in America was like. In a similar vein, a bush-wise safari guide was of special interest to an aging American professor.

Specifically, I wanted to learn more about Africa and the African bush and realized that these guides held the nuggets of information for which I was searching. All in all, it was a match made in bush heaven.

These guides compose an interesting, jovial lot. Each can "spin a yarn" with the best of storytellers. This ability to tell a good tale leads to better tips, and tips are one of the reasons these folks work.

A favorite topic for the guides involved stories about taking tourists into the bush in safari vehicles. These vehicles are open-aired, with the sides of the vehicles unprotected. The back of the vehicle is elevated. Often, though, a tourist will sit beside the driver, especially when business is good. This setup almost guarantees surprising experiences.

One of the more interesting moments involved a safari driver who had an elderly woman sitting beside him during a tour. The group came upon a herd of cape buffalo, animals that can appear calm but are notoriously mean-spirited. The driver wanted his visitors to get a better view of the herd, so he backed the vehicle into the bush with the intention of turning around. As often happens when driving in the bush, the vehicle became stuck. The herd moved toward the truck, and the driver told everyone to be extremely still. The cape buffalo examined the vehicle and its occupants closely. One even ventured toward the passenger side of the vehicle and came face-to-face with the elderly woman sitting there. She remained frozen like a statue as the animal placed its face within inches of her own. She later reported that she could feel the heat coming from the animal's nostrils. Then, after about ten seconds, the cape buffalo turned and walked away. No harm done, except the woman was traumatized.

Immediately after recounting this story, the guide assumed an air of outrage and asked everyone in the television room the following question: "Do you know how she thanked me for this experience? Do you know what she wanted?" Then, before anyone could answer, he answered himself: "A refund!"

Then, with increased effrontery, he continued: "Can you believe that? This woman wanted a refund after I gave her a once-in-a-lifetime experience!" Finally, assuming an air of righteous indignation, the safari guide closed by observing, "I told her for an experience like that she should pay double."

Over the years, I have noticed a strong camaraderie among the guides. They assist one another in a number of different ways. They willingly tell one another where animals, such as lions and leopards, are located. This information is important because it affects tips. "Nothing like a pride of lions near the end of a tour to guarantee a two-hundred-rand tip," one once observed. On another level, the guides share anecdotes, stories, and jokes as well. Hence, the teller might be different, but the story is amazingly similar. I have heard versions of the cape buffalo story with a hippo, a rhino, and a wildebeest coming up to the old woman's face. Perhaps it is just coincidence. But the guides will tell you that a good story needs to be shared with as many tourists as possible.

As I became comfortable with the guides, I began watering the seed that was growing in my mind. I wanted to approach a wild African elephant. The guides encouraged me to do so and were more than willing to offer advice on how to do it. Here is what they suggested:

STEP #1: FIND AN ELEPHANT

Each guide offered this tidbit of advice. Interestingly, each found the observation extremely funny. Each guide who offered this advice laughed and laughed after sharing this piece of bush wisdom.

STEP #2: LOOK AWAY; NEVER STARE!

Once you find an elephant, don't look at it directly. You have to look down and away. If necessary, glance occasionally in the elephant's direction. In essence, once you see the elephant, you cannot let it see you seeing it.

Control of the visual field is important. Elephants, as well as other non-predatory animals, interpret staring as a threat. Predators stare. For your own safety, and for the comfort of the elephant, it is best not to have the elephant think you are a predator. So look away; don't stare.

STEP #3: WATCH THE ELEPHANT CAREFULLY

This step obviously contradicts Step #2, yet it is important to abide by both steps. The key to executing this third step is to glance frequently at the elephant. Your intent is to determine whether it is safe to approach the elephant.

The focus of your attention needs to be on a particular part of the elephant—the space between the ear and the eye. Hidden here, on both sides of the elephant's head, is a temporal gland that oozes fluid when the animal is stressed. Both the males and the females have the gland. Some debate exists about why the elephants secrete fluids through the gland. Recent research has determined that there are different levels of viscosity to the fluid depending on the elephant's level of contentment. However, there is no debate about elephants in musth or those undergoing significant stress: these elephants definitely secrete fluids through their temporal glands. Hence, if you see fluids coming from these glands, NEVER TRY TO APPROACH THAT ELEPHANT. LEAVE. GET OUT OF THERE IMMEDIATELY.

Another warning sign also needs to be watched for: a wiggling leg. If an elephant is walking, its legs are obviously in motion and the movement is not a problem. However, if the elephant is not in motion but is still shaking or wiggling one of its legs, then that elephant is giving you a second visual clue that it is disturbed. So if you see that wiggling foot, then the same advice applies—LEAVE AS FAST AS POSSIBLE.

Other, less obvious signs of disturbance include the following: head shaking, creating a popping sound by slapping its ears against its body, and lifting objects such as branches and throwing them in your direction. The guides warned that elephants can toss objects with amazing accuracy. Be careful of any elephant that exhibits this behavior.

STEP #4: SLOWLY, VERY SLOWLY, BEGIN TO APPROACH THE ELEPHANT

If the elephant exhibits none of the aforementioned behaviors, then you can slowly begin your approach. During this time you must keep your head down, never looking at the elephant directly, but pay careful attention to everything the elephant is doing.

An interesting point emerged in many of the safari guides' descriptions about how to make the approach. In a nutshell, the guides insist that not looking at the elephant involves more than just not imitating a predatory stare. Instead, native African wisdom insists that not looking represents your acknowledgement of the elephant's superiority. "Elephants don't like arrogance," one guide observed. He further suggested that having total humility was the only way that an approach would be successful.

Humility in front of an elephant is not that difficult. One feels extremely minor and unimportant when standing in front of an animal that is three meters high, weighs over five tons, and can run at speeds up to forty kilometers per hour. Additionally, the elephant's aforementioned social skills, empathy for others, and overall perceptiveness make it an animal whose traits are in many ways superior to our own.

A second quality the guides promoted was courage. "You can't be afraid," multiple guides told me. "Elephants can sense fear. They don't want to be around it. It frightens them as well. To an elephant, fear indicates that something unpredictable could happen. They don't like that risk."

Being humble in front of an elephant is easy. Being courageous is an entirely different matter. Practice in and familiarity with the setting seemed the only way to muster my courage. I was practicing in a familiar setting, but I wasn't making much progress.

STEP #5: WATCH THE EARS

If it has not already done so, the elephant will notice you at some point during the approach. When it does so, it will stick out its ears. At this point you should pause and stop moving forward. Some guides recommend bending down a little. They recommend positioning yourself halfway between standing straight and seeming to kneel. Obviously, this pose makes you appear even more humble. It also makes you more vulnerable since this position limits your ability to escape.

Interestingly, the guides acknowledged the risks of lowering yourself in front of the elephant and defended it as an act of courage. Courage, curiously, is a companion of humility.

STEP #6: WITHSTAND THE MOCK CHARGE

Here is the most challenging step in the process; it makes all other actions seem like a piece of cake. As you enter into the elephant's space, it will do one of two things. First, it may just turn and leave. If so, there is nothing you can do about that.

On the other hand, the elephant may do a mock charge to drive you away. The charge consists of the elephant running right at you with its ears fully extended and its trunk raised above its head, and for dramatic effect, the elephant will often let out a shrill, loud bellow. Your job is to hold your ground. The elephant, the guides promise, will stop when it is three to five meters away.

STEP #7: CLEAN YOUR PANTS

Remember, these guides have a sense of humor. Actually, the guides clarify this point by noting that if you make it to step #7, the elephant should stop charging and acknowledge that you have earned the right to be in its presence. And you will be as close as you can safely be—again, somewhere between three and five meters apart.

"What happens if the elephant doesn't stop?" I asked one of the guides describing this process to me.

"No one has ever reported that happening," the guide chuckled in response, fully cognizant of the double entendre he was making.

"How can I tell the difference between a mock and a real charge?" I asked another, although as soon as I asked the question, I knew the answer. But before I could withdraw the question, he replied, "In a mock charge the elephant stops. In a real charge it doesn't." The room then filled with laughter at my expense. I joined in.

Finally, I asked one of the guides if he had ever approached an elephant on foot. Through another swirl of laughter, I heard the response I expected: "Hey, we don't have to have done it to know that it works."

Another guide chimed in: "Priests offer marriage counseling, don't they? None of them have ever been married, right? Just regard us as the pastors of the bush."

It is important to add that each offered the same additional closing piece of advice: Be Careful. That advice made sense.

CHAPTER THREE

Never Run—Unless You Have To

You miss 100% of the shots you don't take.
—Wayne Gretzky

An opportunity to put the safari guides' advice into practice occurred soon after these conversations with them concluded. A herd of eleven elephants showed up in the backyard of the bush house. The herd had two babies, four adolescents, and five adults. I heard them coming through the reeds as I was sitting on the back stoep. After about forty-five minutes, the entire herd was safely ensconced beneath the trees on the Kruger side of the fence. I knew that the time to try out the advice had arrived.

Dear Dan and Laura,

A herd of elephants showed up early this afternoon. Mom was taking a nap, so it seemed like a good time to test the validity of the advice I've received about how to approach an elephant. Here's how the test went.

The first step, Find an Elephant, was taken care of the moment the elephants arrived. However, I didn't want to approach the entire herd, especially since two tiny babies were present. I still have many lessons to learn about living in the bush, but one that I already know is to never get between a mother and her baby.

I waited and watched as the herd lollygagged around in the backyard. The babies remained close to two of the adults, so I stayed away from those elephants.

Eventually, the largest elephant wandered off to the side. It was isolating itself. The size of the elephant inclines me to think it was a male; however, I wasn't able to verify that information visually. (How's that for delicacy?) For descriptive purposes, let's call it a "he."

When the elephant got about ten meters away from other members of the herd, I grabbed my walking stick and started my approach. It was exhilarating!

I first walked parallel to the fence until I was directly aligned with the elephant. It seemed unwise to sneak up on him from the side. No need to scare him.

When I got in position to make my approach, he was twenty meters away. More specifically, I was in Sabie Park and was ten meters away from the fence; the elephant was in the Kruger and was ten meters from the fence. It's important to acknowledge that the fence was between us. The fence provided some level of psychological protection to me—even though it is dilapidated.

As the guides instructed, I lowered my eyes and started slowly approaching the elephant. Full confession, as I started this approach, I glanced at the elephant's temporal glands to check for fluid, at its feet to check for nervous gestures, and at nearby trees for protection. To my thinking, these trees were insurance policies just in case the fence didn't stop him.

I walked forward about five meters before the elephant noticed me. This recognition occurred just as the guides said it would: the elephant stuck out its ears. But even though I anticipated this action, I was shocked by the size of the ears. Each was enormous! And when extended simultaneously, the ears made the elephant's head look like a prehistoric monster. I was a bit taken aback.

At this juncture I didn't execute the guides' advice as well as I should have. Remember, I was supposed to look down and away, but I couldn't. The overall girth of the elephant, especially with the size of those ears attached to that massive head, mesmerized me. I simply stared directly at the elephant. I didn't mean to keep staring, but it was impossible to stop.

The elephant responded exactly as the guides said it would. He trumpeted loudly, raised his trunk, and started to charge toward me. But there is a huge chasm between being told that an elephant will charge and actually experiencing the elephant charging at you. The immediate question that pops into mind is: "Will he stop?" Another question follows immediately: "What if this elephant doesn't know about mock charges?" The bottom line is that when the elephant began its charge, I threw my stick on the ground and ran away like a frightened school girl. Much to my embarrassment, I even screamed as I ran away.

To make matters worse, I forgot about the protection afforded by the nearby trees and darted straight back to the bush house. I didn't even stop when I got to the back stoep. I ran inside and locked the sliding door. If our beds weren't built on a brick base, I would probably have tried to crawl under them as well.

All in all, not my finest moment. Approaching an elephant may take more work than I envisioned.

More later. Right now, I have to go clean my trousers. (Just joking.)

I hope you folks are well.

With love,

Dad, the Elephant Runner

The next day I returned to the television room at the Protea and shared my experience with the safari guides. I might have portrayed myself as being a bit braver than I actually was. But even with a tad bit of self-aggrandizement—for instance, I didn't mention my schoolgirl screams—the story clearly conveyed my fear. I even admitted to running away.

To my surprise, the guides were amazingly supportive. No one teased or made fun of what I had tried to do. Instead, the guides reassured me that it was going to take time to learn to approach an elephant. They even told me to expect to run away many more times. "It's okay to back away and get out of there," one said. "Running away gives you a chance to come back and try again. Stay at the wrong time and you won't get that chance." That observation seemed sensible.

These efforts to approach elephants continued over the next three years. During this time, I continued to read about elephants and listened to whoever would talk to me about elephants and the African bush. I learned, for example, never to approach young elephants that are not associated with a herd. These solitary, adolescent elephants are often in musth—yes, I did see the dripping fluid on occasion—and any movement toward them is very dangerous. I also learned that the best way to identify the gender of an African elephant is by the shape of its head rather than by the presence—or lack thereof—of a male appendage. Heads of females are rounded, while those of males are square. The male appendage actually disappears into the body, except when it is needed.

I also learned a lot about how elephants function together in established family units, demonstrate emotions, love one another, mourn their dead, and communicate with one another. These acts of communication occur not just through trumpeting but also through a gurgle-like sound emitted from their stomachs, as well as through sounds sent at decibel levels imperceptible to the human ear. Elephants even gather information through their feet. All in all, they're a fascinating and highly advanced species.

Yet, even with all the reading, learning, and studying that I undertook, I was unable to approach an elephant successfully. Oftentimes, the elephant wanted nothing to do with me and turned and walked away. On other occasions, I reached the point of the mock charge, but at that stage self-preservation outmaneuvered courage. Each time the elephant charged, my mind posed the same question: What if this elephant doesn't know about mock charges? Then, immediately thereafter, my feet took control, and my body headed swiftly to the safety of the bush house.

A couple of interesting experiences did occur during this period of failed approaches. In one instance, a herd of fifteen elephants wandered into the Kruger backyard but appeared unsettled, almost nervous. The herd was moving back and forth in a manner we had never previously seen. Additionally, many of the elephants were making lots of noise.

Eventually, one of the elephants left by going along the fence in the direction of the Kruger Gate. Usually, I would have followed her and attempted another approach, but on this occasion the nervousness of the herd was too palpable. Sally advised me not to follow, and I abided by her advice. We stayed and watched the herd together.

The other elephants remained in the area but continued to move back and forth restlessly. During most backyard visits, the elephants stop walking and instead just stand and eat the reeds or the leaves from the tree branches. All of these elephants just kept pacing. None were eating.

After about ten minutes, the elephant that had left returned. But this time she was not alone. Following her was a very, very tiny baby. The baby was wet. In all likelihood, the mother had just given birth.

On another occasion, a herd of seventeen elephants showed up at the fence late one morning. Here is what happened:

Dear Dan and Laura,

Our plans for Sunday were to take a long, leisurely drive through the Kruger. We planned to exit through the Malelane Gate and then spend the night in Mbombela, the city that used to be called Nelspruit. Mbombela is about ninety minutes south of Sabie Park. As a treat, we planned to get a hotel room with electricity and a bathtub. One needs to indulge in life's luxuries occasionally.

We were packed and ready to go when suddenly we noticed zebra in the driveway. I don't know what drew them to the area, but for whatever reason a herd of nine zebra and a number of impala, a duiker, and various other animals chose to graze beside our driveway about three meters from the house. We watched them for over an hour. Most fascinating.

We then realized that we had to get going if we were going to tour the Kruger, so we went in to check that the doors and windows were closed. But as I was shutting the sliding door in the back of the house, I heard the heavy crackling of bush. That crackle means elephants are nearby. I found Mom, and we agreed to wait and see if anything came to the fence. We've had many elephants in the backyard this trip. Occasionally, we only hear but don't see them; at other times they appear at a distance; and sometimes, when we are fortunate, they come rather close. This was one of those fortunate times.

The herd was large—probably seventeen or more elephants. One was a very tiny baby—I don't think it was even a meter in height. Two other young elephants were between one and two meters high. We watched the elephants spread out across the area. Some came within centimeters of the fence.

I should add for clarification that I did not make any effort to approach the elephants. Partially it was because we were planning to leave, but even more importantly, my success rate had been so dismal that it seemed time to "give it a rest." Plus, Mom is getting a bit tired of my efforts. So instead, we just watched and enjoyed the visit.

The herd stayed in the area for about thirty minutes. Eventually, the elephants gradually began to disperse. The main portion of the herd moved away from the house toward the hills along the Sabie River that are directly across from our house. Others moved west toward the Kruger Gate and the Protea Hotel. We were left with just a few stragglers eating their last bits before departing.

Then, from a distance, we heard loud trumpeting. The sound came from the direction of the Protea Hotel. Our first thought was that hotel was having an afternoon show. But the volume of the trumpeting continued to increase, and it was quickly obvious that the noise was coming toward us. We waited and listened. After about a minute, a female elephant appeared on the top of the hills and was running and driving two young elephants toward the herd. These were the two elephants that were between one and two meters high.

Then, suddenly, we heard a loud, deep, earth-shattering roar. Mom and I froze. The sound came from the middle of a set of nearby reeds. We looked at each other and simultaneously said, "Lion!" He roared three more times while the mother elephant kept trumpeting and pushing those babies toward the main herd that was still along the Sabie River. The hills obstructed some of our views. But the sounds were unmistakable—roars and trumpets. The silence of the bush was broken.

We soon noticed the entire herd coming together in a circle. They were about fifty meters from the house. The herd pushed the two younger elephants into the middle of the circle. We never saw the young baby.

The trumpeting now stopped, and the herd remained in a tight circle for about five minutes. The roaring also ceased. All of the elephants stood there. None were eating; none were moving. The silence of the bush returned, only now there was a tension accompanying it.

Eventually the circle broke up and the entire herd moved east toward Sabie Park's picnic area. All of the elephants were walking in a direction opposite from the lion's roar.

We never saw the baby elephant again. Nor did we hear any more from the lion.

What a day! We did not make it to Mbombela. Who needs electricity when you have elephants?

I hope you folks are well.

Love,
Dad, the Elephant Observer

I went to see Gat-Jan, the Sabie Park game manager at the time, the day after this incident. I asked him if he thought the lion had killed the very small elephant. Gat-Jan replied with a question: "Did you hear sounds that indicated the lion and the elephant were fighting?"

"No," I replied, "it sounded more as if the lion was threatening the elephant and the elephant was marshaling her forces for protection."

"Then the lion probably didn't hurt the baby elephant," Gat-Jan replied. "If he had tried to kill the baby, you would have heard louder noises and an obvious fight between the two. No mother elephant is going to let a lion kill and eat her baby without putting up a really good fight.

"And in situations such as this," Gat-Jan added, "the mother elephant will usually take down the lion." Sometimes Africa repeats its lessons: never get between a mother and her baby, even if you're a lion.

I continued talking to the safari guides at the Protea during the years of failed elephant approaches. Guides move frequently from one location and one business to another. Therefore, the actual guides with whom I was interacting changed often. But the advice remained consistent: "Don't give up," "Just keep trying," and "Be careful!"

Interestingly, each safari guide insisted that I should be neither discouraged nor embarrassed about backing away during the mock charge. "The elephant and you need to form a relationship," one guide explained. "You will know when you have that relationship."

Another suggested that at some point I would feel secure standing still during a charge and would have no desire to run. "You'll know when it is safe to stay there," this guide added.

Finally, a third safari guide advised that I should "hang in there."

"When the moment is right," he added, "you'll know it."

The advice seemed sound. The likelihood that it would ever occur seemed remote. For whenever an elephant charged, I ran away.

CHAPTER FOUR

A Postage-Stamp View of Africa

The ache for home lives in all of us. The safe place
where we can go as we are and not be questioned.
—Maya Angelou, *All God's Children Need Traveling Shoes*

In *The Innocents Abroad*, Mark Twain describes his journey to Europe and then to the Holy Land. Twain takes pleasure throughout the book in poking fun at people who visit a country for a day or two and promptly become experts in the area.

Most of us are, at one time or another, guilty of these kinds of unwarranted generalizations. In my own case, I once spent two days in St. Petersburg, Russia, and soon thereafter caught myself pontificating to friends about Russia, Russian history, and the Russian economy.

Arrogance sneaks in at the most unsuspecting moments. The mixture becomes especially odious when arrogance unites with a hidden desire to be an authority.

People with a humble nature avoid this combination. They remember that each of us sees the world from our own rather narrow perspective. We can still generalize from our experiences, but we also humbly remember that our view is limited by and built on our private base of experience.

Sabie Park, along with our bush house and its surroundings, provides the setting for our story. Along with the Kruger, these locations represent the sites from which our views of Africa and the African bush emerge. Still, these locations are only postage stamps on the African continent. So while we may generalize broadly about the African bush from these sites, we must also humbly admit that these generalizations spring from a small sample area.

Sabie Park is a 348-hectare private nature reserve. Two sides of the reserve border Kruger Park. A third side borders a highway, and a fourth side borders a burnt-out orange grove. This latter area is undergoing refurbishment and is supposed to emerge soon as a high-end bush camp. But this is Africa, so we will see what happens.

Sabi Sand Game Reserve—a 650-square-kilometer high-end game reserve that borders Kruger to the west—is across the highway from Sabie Park. Sabi Sand caters to wealthy patrons from around the world. It has a private airstrip and luxury lodges, and provides a comfortable safari experience for clients willing to pay dearly for it. Sabi Sand clients are chauffeured from the airport to the lodge, fed first-class meals, and taken on well-managed safaris. One wonders what Twain would have said about the perspectives on Africa afforded by these experiences.

Sabie Park has none of the aforementioned luxuries. It is a bushveld retreat, not a holiday resort. Local covenants restrict noise and require that none of the homes can connect to an energy grid. This restriction means Sabie Park is amazingly quiet. The hum of air conditioners is heard neither during the day nor in the evening. Covenants also restrict how much time an owner can live in a bush house. The current rule is that an owner can spend up to 118 nights a year in Sabie Park. The idea behind this restriction is that it protects the bush from being overused.

A wire fence surrounds the entire area. As previously mentioned, the fence that borders the Kruger is meant to keep lions and elephants from entering. The fence that borders the highway and the orange grove is meant to keep out strangers and unregistered guests. First-time visitors to South Africa are often surprised that most houses are surrounded either by a fence or by an imposing cement wall. Often, the fence is electrified and the wall is topped off with an electric wire as well as a barbed-wire line to discourage people from climbing over it. Sabie Park is protected like these locations.

Everyone must pass through a gated area to enter Sabie Park. The moment you enter, you see a tennis court, a swimming pool, and a pleasant garden area to which members can retreat. These amenities are the only vestige of upscale living that you will see in the area. For as soon as you begin traveling down the dusty roads, you realize that you are going into an area that is bushveld, not a country club.

The roads in Sabie Park are hilly, surrounded by trees and thick bush, and, to no one's surprise, very African. All are dirt-covered and filled with bumps and occasional trenches. The bumps and trenches restrict one's speed and protect the animals that roam about freely. While driving along on the road, you are likely to see giraffes, zebras, wildebeests, impalas, warthogs, and kudus. Recently a nyala moved in by jumping the fence that borders the Kruger.

Sabie Park contains close to one hundred bush houses, each of which has an erf number assigned to it. Ours is Erf 286. The erf label comes from the Afrikaans and means "a plot of land." Originally, the word in Dutch meant "an inheritance." As a reminder, we did not inherit this location.

Each house in Sabie Park also has a name displayed on the driveway. Many of the names refer to local animals. Thus, names such as Hornbill Hollow, Giraffe, and Gecko are easy to spot. Other names imply remoteness: Woodlands, Allora ("Then") and, Tydloos ("Timeless"). And, of course, some imply a fun, carefree lifestyle—Hakuna Matata sits close to the entrance to Sabie Park. It is important to add that none of the staff call any of the bush houses by their respective names. Staff members simply use the numbers. So our bush house is Erf 286.

The previous owner of our bush house named it *Xilowa*. I asked what the name meant and learned the word derived from Zulu. None of the staff knew its exact meaning. A check on Google Translate revealed that there is no such word. However, *ilowa* means "that" in Zulu. The word also means "enter" in Nyanja, an appropriate word for the beginning of a driveway. Nyanja, by the way, is a Bantu language spoken mostly in Malawi, Zambia, and Mozambique. Each country is classified as being within sub-Saharan Africa.

No matter what *Xilowa* means, however, staff members were quick to point out that the use of Zulu or Nyanja is offensive to some of the Sabie Park employees. The staff working in Sabie Park are mostly Tsonga. The Zulus, the Nyanja, and the Tsonga have not been the best of friends over the years, even though their tribes are closely related. It's rather like trying to explain to an outsider why it is in "bad taste" to wear a shirt proclaiming allegiance to Auburn or Tennessee while walking around on the University of Alabama campus. Similarly, one should think twice about wearing a Michigan State or Ohio State outfit on the University of Michigan campus. An outsider would ask, "But aren't those schools in the same conference? Aren't they geographically close?" The answer is, "Yes, but it's complicated."

We took steps to rename the house as soon as we learned that *Xilowa* offended the Tsonga staff. We bought and planted a new sign that declares the new name: "Ron and Sally's Bush House." The sign offends no one, although it does elicit a few chuckles from the Tsonga staff. I guess they don't hear the power in the name.

The houses in Sabie Park reside on stands. A stand is a plot of land. The stands range in size from one to four hectares. The bush between the houses is often deep. As a result, most houses are isolated.

Our house is particularly isolated. Arguably, it is the most isolated house in Sabie Park. Nothing but the Kruger is nearby. This isolated location means that driving to the house is almost as exciting as being there. We learned about this excitement the first time we drove to the house. Even though it occurred more than thirteen years ago, I remember the experience as though it was yesterday.

Dear Dan and Laura,

We are here. We drove from Pretoria yesterday and are staying in a rondavel in Skukuza. A rondavel is a small one-room hut. Skukuza, as you may remember, is the largest rest camp in the Kruger. It is a fifteen-minute drive from Skukuza to Sabie Park. Our plans for today and tomorrow are to buy furniture for the house and then move in.

Let's begin the story of our bush adventure with the arrival. What an arrival it was.

You both know that I am an inherently optimistic person. Optimism is part of my makeup. I almost always believe good will win and right will conquer all. "Now wait a minute, Dad," you ask, "what does your mental condition have to do with arriving at the bush house?"

"Everything," I answer, "because yesterday I flirted with the dark side of the coin: depression. It is not a pleasant host." Let me clarify.

After arriving yesterday, we checked into a hotel in Centurion—a suburb of Pretoria. I don't know what caused my mind to enter the doldrums, but it did. Thirty-two hours of travel could have contributed to the problem. In any case, as soon as we arrived at the hotel, I went into a mental funk and decided that buying this bush house was a huge mistake.

I started asking myself questions I should have asked earlier: "Why did we buy a house on the internet?" "Why did we buy a house that no one we trust had ever even entered?" "Why did we buy a house in South Africa?" I even began questioning Lonnie Strickland and Mike Crosbie's assessment that the area was safe. In Africa, safe means from people, not from animals. Who knows what animal might enter the house and eat us!

My mental condition worsened as I answered each of the questions with the same refrain: "It's because I am a stupid, naïve, cockeyed optimist," I wailed. "And now," I cried further, "that optimism is going to cost us wheelbarrows full of money."

I convinced myself that the house had to have a serious defect. The depression and wailing continued throughout the night and into the light of morning as we left for Sabie Park. The drive takes five hours, and my mental state became darker the closer we got to the destination. But as the depression worsened, it focused on one item: the fact that no one we trusted had ever been inside the house.

I was certain that a house existed in Sabie Park—Lonnie and Mike had at least seen a structure. But I was equally certain that the house had a terrible odor in it. I convinced myself that someone or something had died in the house, remained in it for weeks, if not months or years, and that the stench could never be removed. That was why the real estate agent had supposedly brought the wrong key: she didn't want Lonnie and Mike to smell the stench. "I should have thought of that earlier," I lamented, "but my naïve optimism believed the realtor when she said she made a mistake with the key." "I am an optimistic fool," I chided myself while driving.

Sabie Park is surrounded by a fence and has a gated entrance that everyone must pass through to enter the area. We drove up to the gate and introduced ourselves to the guard, Solly. He seemed nice. Solly instructed us to go to the main office to meet the manager, get the key, and get registered as owners. We did that, and met the property managers, Cheryl and her husband, Gat-Jan. Both seemed nice as well. They gave us a map with directions to the house and promised to stop by to check on us in a little while.

The depression eased slightly after meeting Cheryl and Gat-Jan. Both seemed reputable, and neither mentioned an odor in the house. Plus, the promise to come to check on us seemed positive. If the house stank too much, why would they come to visit?

So we began the bumpy, dusty half-mile drive to the house. We left on a path named Maroela.

As soon as we got onto Maroela, we saw an ostrich. "Now, that's cool," I said to Mom. Apparently, we later learned from Gat-Jan, ostriches can get mean. So we won't go too close to him. We also learned that it is a myth that ostriches stick their heads in the sand when frightened. Instead, they attack. Our education begins.

But I digress. Back to the drive. We drove silently along Maroela, looking to see what we could see. Suddenly, after a few minutes, we saw a herd of wildebeest grazing beside the road. "Now that's cool too," I said to Mom. We stopped briefly to look at the wildebeests. They didn't want to be observed, so they sauntered off into the bush and disappeared. Although I was still convinced that we had made a mistake in buying a house sight unseen, I was becoming pleased that we had bought the house in Sabie Park. If nothing else, we could buy a tent and camp in the backyard. That is, of course, if the odor from the house didn't drift outside.

We continued along Maroela, went down one hill, up another, and soon encountered four zebra standing beside the road. We stopped to look at them. They didn't seem to mind being watched, as evidenced by the fact that they stared right back at us. Their look seemed to ask, "And who are you to be visiting here?" I guess they viewed us as foreigners. We are.

We next took a sharp right turn onto a road named Gwarieboos and headed down a road with an open plain area. I was looking to the sides to see if anything else was visible when Mom suddenly shouted, "Look what is in the road!" That was the one place I had not been looking.

Believe it or not, standing in the middle of the road were three giraffes, two females and one male. They towered over us. I got out of the car to take a picture, and they turned and looked at me in confusion. They seemed mildly annoyed, stared at us for a moment, and then returned to eating from the top of a tall tree whose leaves make it flat on the top. We had to wait ten minutes for them to finish eating and get out of the road. Time is flexible in Africa.

We next turned left on a road called Appalblaar. The bush gets thicker and the trees a little larger in this area. As a result, the setting becomes darker since the sunlight is unable to fight its way through the top of the trees. It was a mite spooky.

At long last we got to our driveway. And what a driveway it is. The driveway is a dirt path that goes sharply downhill through a thicket of bushes that knock against your car and scratch your windows. There are huge boulders in different parts of the driveway. The house is close to the Sabie River, so the driveway is basically a path toward the river.

As we wound our way down the path, my depression returned with a vengeance. Nothing this remote could be good. As we twisted and turned our way toward the house, I even became afraid that Lonnie and Mike had been duped. What if the house was a removable structure that had been set up and then taken down? If so, we were about to pay the price for their naïveté. Then, suddenly, we turned around one final bend and there it was: our African bush house.

The outside of the house is brick with a thatch roof. The thatch is brown and dark from years of weathering. There is no electricity, but there is solar power. The solar power panels sit in the back of the house toward the driveway. You drive under a deck that protrudes over the back of the house and creates a nice parking space. We drove right in.

By this point, panic, fear, depression, and anxiety had totally overtaken both of us. The excitement of the animal sightings evaporated. I was again convinced that we had been ripped. A house was present, no doubt about that. It was even rather attractive for a bush house. But the stench inside was going to be mind-boggling.

So, after a pause and a long, deep breath, I pulled the key from my pocket and we headed for the back door. The key fit and the door opened. Sniffing like a bloodhound, I entered the house. Amazingly, it smelled . . . like nothing! There was no odor. It was just a normal-smelling house. The house smelled a bit musty from having been closed for a while, but the odor was nothing that a few minutes of open windows couldn't remove. It smelled . . . GOOD!!!

I turned to Mom and said, "Whew." She seemed confused, an appropriate response since I had never shared my fears with her.

We then proceeded to scope out the house. I'll describe it for you in a later note. For now, just know that at the back of the house is a sliding-glass door. And there, I mean right there, no more than twelve yards away, is the Kruger. So wild animals can come within twelve yards of our house! There is a thin wire fence separating our yard from the Kruger. The fence is supposed to be electrified, but I kind of have my doubts. It looks in disrepair. We'll find out later whether it is electrified or not.

One more essential feature of the house: the boma. The

boma is an area to the side of the house where we will cook. The boma is outside and surrounded by a cane fence. In the middle of the boma is a raised area on which we will prepare our meals; that raised area is called a lapa. The lapa is constructed of concrete and brick. It is one meter high, one meter wide, and five meters long. Beside the lapa is a magnificent tree that towers over the entire area. It might be a marula tree—or it might be a jackalberry. I don't know my trees that well. I will tell you, though, that that sucker is huge!!!

We looked around a bit, but it was getting late, and we had to get to Skukuza by 5:30. So we took off. Day 1 concluded: odorless.

I hope you folks are well.

Love,
Dad, the Blood Hound–Sniffing House Detective

CHAPTER FIVE

Keep the Doors Locked and the Windows Closed

'Home is the place where, when you have to go there,
They have to take you in.'
'I should have called it
Something you somehow haven't to deserve.'
—Robert Frost, "The Death of the Hired Man"

Our Sabie Park bush house is pretty much a typical low-end bush house. Fancier bush houses reside in the area. Ours is noted more for its isolated location beside the Kruger than for its design or spacious interior.

The main entrance to the house is through a carport. A door in the back of the carport leads to a great room that has a kitchen and a living area. The great room, in fact the entire house, has a tile floor and a thatch roof. The great room's total area is about 150 square meters. The thatch roof covers the entire house and slopes dramatically upward toward a peak that is easily fifty meters high.

Two bedrooms are downstairs—one with a queen bed and the other with two twin beds. You enter the bedrooms through doors off the great room. A small loft with a balcony sits upstairs. The loft holds two additional twin beds. The house has two bathrooms, both of which are downstairs. A sliding door at the back of the house opens onto the back stoep. Behind the stoep, as we have mentioned, is the Kruger.

The batteries to which the solar panels are attached can store enough energy to go three days without being charged. After that, we go dark until the sun shines again. Incidentally, no hair dryers are allowed. A hair dryer uses three days of electricity within five minutes. We wash our hair regularly, but it dries au naturel.

The house is equipped with a tiny stove and a small refrigerator, both of which are powered by propane gas. A large dining table made out of railroad ties sits in the center of the great room. Two oak couches and two semi-comfortable chairs make up the sitting/lounge area in the living room.

But to talk about the house in terms of its physical layout does it a disservice. It's the feeling that accompanies the house—and particularly its location in the African bush—that is important. It's about a "Squeeze the Juice" lifestyle, not a surveyor's measuring stick. We learned about the importance of the house's location as soon as we moved in.

Dear Dan and Laura,

We spent our first night in the bush house. Quite a night it was. Let me briefly share two highlights.

First, we had some problems getting the stove and the refrigerator to work. Both operate with propane. I asked for help from the management and they sent someone late in the day—about 18:00. By that time it was dark—remember, it's winter here. Our initial plan was to cook steaks on the lapa and use the stove for potatoes. However, it took a bit of time for the repairman to get the stove operating. It was about 19:00 by the time he finished. I then politely asked if it was too late to cook outside.

The repairman gave me a puzzled look and asked, "You know there are leopards out there?"

I said, "Yes, I know that, but is it safe to cook outside this late in the night?"

He repeated the question he had asked earlier: "You know there are leopards out there?"

"I understand," I replied again, "but they are out there all the time. Is it—"

At this point the repairman recognized the need to answer directly. He therefore interrupted and said, "No, it is not safe to cook outside this late at night. Do it tomorrow, but start earlier when it is still light."

Then he offered two additional tips. First, when you cook outside at night, surround yourself with fire. Second, no matter what you do at night, always stay close to your fire. Not bad advice, metaphorically speaking. It is also solid practical advice. It seems the animals don't like fire and so go out of their way to avoid it. Note to self: keep the fires lit.

Okay, now the second story, which is rather weird. We decided to eat some leftover sandwiches from our trip. Thus, by 19:45 we had "dined" and cleaned up. There is not a lot to do in the African bush at this point—no television, no computers, no internet. So we decided to read. Even that was a struggle since the solar-powered lights are dim. Also, the quiet is so intense that it is disturbing. But we struggled on.

We read for fifteen minutes. Then, suddenly, I thought I faintly heard a noise. It sounded like beating drums.

I put down my book and tried to listen more closely. But

the sound had disappeared. It was obvious that my imagination was running out of control. I mean, really, drums playing in the African night? This is a really bad movie. I looked at Mom but didn't say anything.

Soon the sound started again. It was definitely drums. I glanced at Mom and noticed she was listening as well. Soon she looked back at me and asked, "Do you hear drums?"

"Yes," I said answered, relieved that my imagination wasn't going totally berserk.

"What do you think it is?" she asked.

"Don't know," I replied. Then I faked confidence and said, "I'm sure we're safe." I was lying. I was so scared that I was shaking. It did not take much perceptiveness to see through my feigned confidence. "Yes," she said, "we're safe unless others don't want us here. Perhaps those drums are signals."

I told her to stop being foolish. I elected not to add that I had been having similar thoughts.

The drum noises lasted for twenty minutes. The noise became increasingly louder and was followed by chanting, shouting, and screaming. By this point, Mom and I were about to jump out of our skin. Then, suddenly, the noise stopped. Silence returned. We heard nothing for the rest of the evening. Needless to say, we didn't sleep too well last night.

The drum mystery got unraveled this afternoon. The Protea Hotel at Kruger Gate is a kilometer directly downriver from us. The hotel is a haven for tourists seeking a bush experience. Six nights a week, the hotel sponsors a show put on by a group of local Tsonga. These folks make extra income by playing the drums and performing traditional tribal dances. Hence, we really did hear drums and shouting. That's a relief.

Later today Lonnie and Kitty Strickland are going to join us for a night. We've asked them to come to give us lessons in Bush Living 101. We should become a little more relaxed once we get our arms around what we are doing here.

I have to admit that I'm looking forward to a good night's sleep once Lonnie is in the house. Not that he'd protect me—I know he wouldn't. But I'm faster than he is. That's all you have to be over here—faster than the next person. I wonder if there is a useful metaphor in there as well?

I hope you folks are well.

Love,
Dad, Sleepless in Sabie

Perhaps the best way to describe the house and its location is to emphasize what is not available. There is no phone service. None! Landlines are not present and there is no cell service. All available cell signals are blocked by the fact that the house sits down a hill beside the Sabie River.

The lack of cell service means there is no internet. We also have no furnace, so there is no heat for the cold. Temperatures will often "dip" close to freezing during the winter months of June and July. We also have no air conditioning for the occasional "spurts" of warmth that surface during South African winters. Guns are not allowed in Kruger or in Sabie Park—so we have none. Nor do we have paved roads or pets.

Finally, there is one more thing we don't have: the ability to leave doors and windows open, unless we are very close by. If we walk away and leave the doors or windows unguarded, baboons will strike with a vengeance. The consequences of such a visit are not pleasant.

Stated simply, baboons are burglars. They are experts at identifying and entering a bush house through an unlocked door or an unlatched window. And once they get in, they become like college students celebrating spring break in a rented beach house. To this day, two of the exposed beams that support the thatch roof in our bush house have deep scratch marks from baboons having swung on them during a successful break-in.

Bush house owners report having had baboon burglars remove food from cupboards and refrigerators, eat some of it, and then throw the rest on the floor. Other owners report having had bedding yanked from beds and tables, and chairs overturned and tossed about the room. But worst of all, and this experience is repeated with every baboon break-in, is the kind of in-your-face defiance with which baboons mark a successful entry. Stated delicately, the baboons spread feces throughout the house. All in all, once you have experienced a baboon break-in, you have a new, but less sympathetic, understanding of the phrase "animal house."

Over the years, we have noticed that unlike elephants, baboons don't remember people from one season to another. Thus, each year when we arrive, the baboons watch us closely and check that the doors and windows are secure when we leave. Sometimes, we drive up the driveway and pretend to leave; then, we turn back and watch as the baboons check out the house. They turn the doorknobs and push on the doors, they pull up and push down on the windows, and, finally, they circle the house looking for any other opening. After a week or two they give up. The baboons award us a passing grade in house security. They still occasionally check in on us, but not with the same level of regularity as when we first arrive.

Baboons have trashed our house unmercifully on three occasions. Once they got in through an unlocked door, once through an unlatched window, and the third and final time through a sliding-glass door that I thought I had locked.

> Dear Dan and Laura,
>
> We arrived safely from Satara late this afternoon. It was a pleasant trip.
>
> Mom was tired after the long drive, so she decided to take a nap. Before she did, I declared my intention to drive to the Protea to connect to the internet. Mom said, "That's fine" as she headed to the bedroom. Then she added, "Just be sure to lock me in."
>
> Following her instructions, I double-checked to make sure the front door was locked. It never occurred to me to check the sliding door at the back of the house. It was closed, so I assumed it was secure. That was a bad assumption.
>
> About forty-five minutes after I left, Mom heard a noise and thought I was back. She then heard baboons beating on the bedroom window and came out to tell me about it. To her surprise, she discovered a baboon standing on top of the refrigerator while three others scampered around the house. Mom was standing in front of the sliding door, so she moved

to the side and screamed, "GET OUT OF HERE." All four left immediately.

Immediately after the foursome left, Mom heard a noise in the loft. A fifth baboon was up there. The baboon wanted to follow its buddies, so he hung from the loft railing and jumped to the floor. That's a three-meter drop. But he wasn't as astute as his buddies. Instead of running through the section of the sliding door that was open, he ran straight into the double windowed segment. Mom said he ran into the window, backed up, looked confused, and ran into it again. After a third try, he looked frustrated and just stood there. Mom was worried that he'd never get out.

To complicate matters further, at this point I drove into the carport. The lights from my car reflected off the sliding-glass windows and startled the baboon even more. Being unable to figure out what to do, he ran back up the steps and retreated into the loft.

Now, don't ask for clarification about this next part of the story. I still don't understand it. I walked into the house and Mom and said, "There is a monkey upstairs. Get him out." Why she called it a monkey I will never know.

Fearing no monkey, I grabbed my walking stick and headed to the loft. When I was halfway up the steps, the baboon jumped to the top of the rail that separates the loft from the steps and began beating his chest like Tarzan. He was huge, at least one and a half meters tall. And standing on the rail above me made him look even larger. I actually thought it was Godzilla. Stated simply, that baboon scared the bejeepers out of me.

I shouted an obscenity followed by the observation, "That's not a monkey!" Mom shouted back, "Just get him out!" At that moment the baboon complied by jumping from the top rail of the loft down to the main floor. That jump is at least four meters down. Again, though, the sliding-glass door puzzled him. He ran into the window two more times! Finally, he noticed the darkness that had set in on the other side of the sliding door and scooted out the open segment.

The final damage report: a dozen oranges ruined, a box of

tangerines gone, a pack of bananas eaten, tables and chairs overturned, and pounds of baboon poop all over the house. Just to be clear, most of the feces came from the baboons. That which was on the steps going up to the loft, well, you can guess its source. (Just joking; there was no feces on the steps.)

We cleaned the house and headed for drinks and dinner at the Protea. We had no desire to eat in the house.

After we finished dining at the Protea, we decided to relax for a few minutes in the television room. That's where I'm writing this note. I had left my laptop in the car so I went to get it while Mom settled into the television room couches. On my way to the car, I noticed one of the gate guards standing in the parking lot, shining flashlights between the cars and into the trees. I asked him, "What are you looking for?" He replied, "A cheetah is in the area, and I'm trying to scare it away." I mentioned that we have two leopards in Sabie Park, and he replied, "I know . . . I've heard. But right now I have to get rid of this cheetah."

Just another day in Africa.

I hope you folks are well.

Love,
Dad, Proud Husband of Baboon Sally

The earlier description of the bush house focused on what it doesn't have: electricity, cell phone service, and so forth. What, then, does it have? What draws us back to this site year after year?

That question is easy to answer: quiet, peace, and solitude. The bush house offers a chance to decouple from a modern, totally connected society. It provides an opportunity to disconnect, both literally and figuratively. It provides time and space for reflection. It provides a chance to reconnect with nature, with one another, and with one's self. It is a place to rejuvenate.

Guests report feeling like addicts in withdrawal for the first couple of days in the bush house. The "drugs" of twenty-first-century society—the noise, the rush, and the busyness; the constant need to be available, to be reachable; and even the need to multitask and to be available 24/7—take days to detox and evaporate from our systems. Once these disappear guests can truly begin to experience the African bush. It is then that they can sit in solitude on the back stoep, look at the Kruger, and feel no need to know what is happening elsewhere. That feeling is strangely self-sufficient. I suspect the strangeness comes from the realization of how little we really need to survive. That realization is simultaneously humbling and invigorating.

After achieving the state of "needing nothing," our guests begin to see with humble eyes. Instead of needing to know and be involved with what is going on in the office, the nation, or even the world, they begin to notice, appreciate, and care about birds sitting in nearby trees. They also observe different grasses and even the different light that Africa lends to the earth, especially at sunset. These things are important to see and appreciate.

And, of course, our guests observe and begin to look forward to visits from various animals that appear at the backyard fence. These visitors range from herds of elephant to Cape buffalo, kudu, impala, bushbucks, monkeys, and baboons. If our guests are fortunate, a lion or a leopard may appear as well. And if they look out early in the morning, they may occasionally see a hippo walking beside the fence. Each animal approaches the setting with caution, studies us earnestly, and then decides whether we have developed the appropriate level of humble appreciation for this setting. If we have, they are apt to stay in the area for a while; if not, they leave quickly.

Humility is not just mandatory when approaching an elephant; it is also the best way to see 90 percent of animals in the bush. Antelopes such as kudu, impala, and bushbuck and mammals such as giraffe, wildebeest, and zebra will look at and study us deeply once they notice our presence. A humble, subservient gaze downward is the appropriate response to their examination. We must remain calm, quiet, composed, and non-threatening. The more humility we emit, the longer the animal will remain in our presence. Also, the more humble we are, the closer the animal will come. There is no need to prove our superiority to these animals. We are not superior here. Just try to walk out and live in the bush without any mechanical protection. These animals do that daily. Even if we take that step, we become only equal to them, not superior. Thus, a call for humility is appropriate.

A different tact is needed to respond to the other 10 percent of the animals. These are the predators and scavengers. Courage is the key to engaging with these animals. We try to never show fear to a predator such as a leopard or a scavenger such as a hyena. We do not want to arrogantly ignore the threat that animal poses, but we also don't want to look too humble either. Instead, we stand straight and look as imposing as possible. It is still advisable not to stare at the animal for too long. Predators interpret staring as a challenge. But it is important to make enough visual contact to show awareness and courage. If we have a walking stick or any other kind of instrument, we place it in both hands and hold it high above our heads. This pose makes us look as large and as intimidating as possible. That's an important pose. Predators size us up. They are determining whether they can take us down. The larger we look, the less likely it is that the predator will engage us.

Finally, and most importantly, we never run from a predator. Quick movements trigger an attack reaction. The consequences of this behavior are not pleasant.

These bush lessons provide important insights for first-time bush visitors. They are, likewise, important reminders to those who have lived here for years. The lessons are similar to friendly reminders to buckle your seat belt on an airplane. Even the most grizzled traveler occasionally forgets to do that, thereby opening themself to needless risk.

Even more importantly, these bush lessons open doors, both figuratively and metaphorically, to other aspects of the bush. Armed with these insights, we can safely step off the back stoep and begin to explore the nearby surroundings. And even though it is only three meters from the sliding door of the bush house to the boma, those three meters reveal an entirely new world of bush experiences.

CHAPTER SIX

A Little Night Music

No wonder of it: sheer plod makes plough down sillion
Shine, and blue-bleak embers, ah my dear,
Fall, gall themselves, and gash gold-vermillion.
—Gerard Manley Hopkins, "The Windhover"

In me thou see'st the glowing of such fire
That on the ashes of his youth doth lie,
As the death-bed whereon it must expire,
Consum'd with that which it was nourish'd by.
—William Shakespeare, "Sonnet 73"

Chapter 6

The boma is a bush patio. It sits beside the bush house and consists of a brick-lined floor, a lapa on which to cook, and the aforementioned cane fence that encircles it to provide pseudo-separation from wild animals. But the physical dimensions of the boma are not what make it special. It is what happens inside the boma that counts. For it is here that a South African rite of passage occurs. It is here that you experience the pleasures of a bush braai. Few events are more important to the bush experience.

Described simply, a braai is a South African barbeque. A bush braai is a South African barbeque that occurs in the bush. The difference is important. In the bush, you hear amazing noises, feel the remoteness of being away from civilization, and have the possibility, but not the probability, of being attacked or eaten by a wild animal. Domestically conducted bush braais have none of these characteristics.

The bush braai is so enjoyable that we have devised a simple formula for explaining it: enjoyment of the bush braai increases proportionately to the number of times you do it. Most other facets of life have a wear-down factor—the pleasure diminishes proportionally to the number of times you engage in the activity. Not the bush braai. It gets better every time you do it.

At the outset, before sharing details about the braai and stories associated with it, we need to acknowledge that every braai is a little bit different. Each person, each family, as well as different locations throughout South Africa, has individual variations that make their braai special. Just as Carnival in Rio is similar to but different from Mardi Gras in New Orleans, and just as Mardi Gras in New Orleans is similar to but different from Mardi Gras in Mobile, so likewise, each South African braai has its own unique characteristics, its own unique traditions, and its own unique flavors. And, of course, just as each location will proclaim its own celebration as the best, so likewise each person enthusiastically argues heartily for the superiority of his or her own braai experience.

So, with this qualification in mind, let us share our own bush braai procedures. And just so you know, ours really is the best.

To begin the braai, we go outside, enter the boma, and light twelve kerosene lanterns. We do this between 17:30 and 18:00 since that is when winter dark begins to overtake the South African bush. The light heightens the atmosphere and simultaneously lets us see what we are doing. It is also not inconsequential that firelight, as we have mentioned before, keeps animals away.

Next, after the lanterns are lit, we stack wood onto the lapa and start the fire. The fire provides warmth as the evening coolness descends. The temperature on most evenings drops dramatically after sunset. Often, by the end of the braai, the temperature will be between 7 and 10 degrees Celsius (42 to 50 degrees Fahrenheit).

Once the fire gets underway, we get wine, cheese, and crackers and proceed to partake in the assorted snacks while monitoring the fire and listening to the bush. Importantly, the fire is also creating burning embers during this phase of the braai. These embers are essential to the cooking that will occur later.

Reasonable amounts of wine are consumed during this "ember" stage of the braai. This consumption occurs both for pleasure and to ameliorate the realization that you are sitting in the remote African bush with leopards, lions, elephants, and rhinoceros. A bit of "liquid courage" never hurts.

But a braai is never about drinking; it is about appreciation. Thus, during this stage of the braai, participants are encouraged to lean back on their chairs, place their feet on the lapa, and listen to the music of the bush. The sounds are amazing. As day transitions to evening, one set of animals, the day animals, bids "goodbye," while another set of animals, the night animals, shouts "hello." Birds chirp, sing, and often seem to shout "good night." Insects, bugs, and other night creatures screech, squawk, and squeal to announce that they are awake and ready for the evening to begin.

But the birds and the bugs provide only the background chorus to the braai's symphony; the true music of the braai begins when distinct sets of animals begin playing their designated roles.

The first and the most raucous sounds come from baboons. These creatures, about which few good things can be said, interrupt the early evening with a series of screeches and screams that indicate a serious argument is taking place. It is. Baboons are day creatures. They live within a distinct hierarchy but challenge one another to get higher within the hierarchy. This tendency is especially prevalent in the early evening, when where you sleep influences your standing. Hence, the baboon sounds you are hearing are a nightly argument about who is going to sleep where. Those in lower positions try to sneak into the positions held by the superiors. The superiors, of course, want to maintain positions of authority and attempt to drive the subordinates into their lower-status locations.

Interestingly, recent research indicates that baboons sleep fitfully. They sit upright in the trees, balance their bottoms on branches, and are easily awakened. A deep, good night's sleep is not something to which baboons are accustomed. It is impossible to sleep soundly when your position in the hierarchy is constantly under attack. It seems as if there might be a lesson here as well.

Shortly after the baboons settle their sleeping arrangements, a low, deep "auhh, auhh, auhhh" emerges from the bush. This sound, which resembles old men laughing at a joke, gets repeated numerous times. These sounds come from a pod of night people—hippos. Hippos make these sounds to declare their locations and to outline their strategic plans for the evening. These plans usually involve foraging the local grounds for various plants to eat. If you are within hearing range of hippo sounds, then you are in an area of gastronomic delight that the hippos consider their domain. Be careful.

A frequently cited bush statistic is that more people are killed by hippos than by any other wild animal. This statistic may or may not be true. It is impossible to find the organization that keeps statistics about African bush deaths. It is, however, true that at night hippos wander in search of food far from their normal river habitats. It is also true that when frightened, hippos run straight toward the nearest body of water. Anything that gets in that path gets run over. So it is solid bush advice to never get between a hippo and a body of water.

Perhaps the best way to understand hippos and their behavior is to think of them as the animal kingdom's midlevel executives. Hippos have vague ideas about where they are going and how they are going to find new food. They therefore amble forth into new territory, eat some grass, deposit some hippo droppings, and then scramble back rapidly and ruthlessly to safety the minute a challenge occurs. Their path going away from the water is meandering and a bit difficult to detect. Hippos tread softly when on their way to eat. But their path going back is easy to detect since it contains trampled grass, broken branches, dead bodies, and a variety of other animals running away in fear.

Hippos become noticeably quieter as the evening progresses. By this point, the darkness of Africa has settled in and overtakes all of the areas outside of the boma. Once darkness has overtaken the setting, a "who who who hoo hoo whoohoo" sound often interrupts the evening's temporary silence. This sound is intriguing since it initially comes from at least two different places in the bush, places that are quite far from one another. But as the evening progresses, the sounds get closer and closer to one another. Eventually, the sounds become one.

The interesting event occurring here is nature ensuring the survival of one of its many prized possessions: the wood owl. One source of these sounds is a male wood owl. This male is courting—or should we say "whooing"?—his female counterpart. The female understands the process. Hence, her initial response to the calls from the male is a "oooohooo." This sound combines an acknowledgement that she hears him with an indication that she might be interested. Put in simple human terms, she is saying, "I hear you. Keep hooting and I'll think about it."

The male responds to her call with an additional set of "whoos" and "hoots" that resemble those he previously emitted. "No sense in varying from what might be working," he seems to think. At this point the female decides whether the two are going to get closer during the evening. If she decides to stop, she is simply quiet. When this happens the male continues to call for a while. Soon, however, he recognizes the meaning of the silence and flies away to wait for another evening.

If the female decides to continue the courting ritual, she shows her interest by flying toward him and answering his call again. But this time she alters her call. Instead of a "ooohoo," it becomes a "who who whoo hoo," which imitates his call. The process is now in motion. The male acknowledges her response by repeating his calls and moving closer and closer as well.

It is enjoyable to sit at the braai and hear these two moving closer and closer together as the evening progresses. Neither is in that much of a rush. Both keep communicating. Eventually, they find one another. When this happens, the whooping becomes raucous. It is amazing to hear and must be a wonderful experience. Go wood owls!

It is important to acknowledge that wood owls are monogamous. They mate for life. Additionally, they have a very intricate but well-documented mating ritual. It begins with the male "playing the fool" and acting obsequious and subservient to the female. Then, given some encouragement to proceed further, he seeks the female's approval through an intricate set of gifts left for her approval. Included in these gifts are dead rats, dead snakes, and dead lizards. A smitten male wood owl spares no effort with his gifts. If the female deems the gifts appropriate, she acquiesces to the male, and the two commit to one another for life.

Yet, despite this established ritual, it is sometimes a bit of innocent fun to join in the festivities in the dark of the evening. As mentioned in a following email, after a glass or two of wine, I sometimes play the role of one of the two partners and try to woo the other to the braai. My success in this venture has been limited, although on a few occasions I have managed to get the owls to fly toward me, at least temporarily. On one occasion I actually saw one of the owls. His look of confusion followed by a look of disgust still sits in my memory. As soon as he realized that he had been duped, he flew off and resumed calling his appropriate partner. Since the pair came back the next evening, I have always assumed that my intervention was nothing but a harmless flirtation.

A final sound that often shows up early in the evening and resurfaces throughout the night is the "whOOOoooOOOP, whOOOoooOOOP, whOOOoooOOOP" of the hyena. Disney's *The Lion King* captures the appearance of these creatures with amazing accuracy. At first glance, hyenas are scary-looking creatures. Their front legs are lower than their back legs, so they give the appearance of being humpbacked. Their coats are spotted, and their heads are elongated almost to a point. Their movements are a mixture of walks and hops.

Over time, you become accustomed to and almost appreciative of the hyena's less-than-appealing appearance. They are fascinating animals. The bite of a hyena is three times as powerful as that of a lion. So we are always careful when one comes nearby. Fortunately, hyenas are seldom aggressive toward humans. In their hearts, they would rather steal from behind our backs than face us.

Hyenas are part-time hunters and full-time scavengers. Forty percent of their food they catch themselves; 60 percent they steal from other animals. True to their scavenger reputations, hyenas sneak up behind the cane poles of the boma looking for opportunities to steal food or other items that interest them. I have, I must confess, almost suffered severe cardiac arrest when on two different occasions a hyena snuck up behind the cane poles of the boma and started to "whoop, whoop, whoop" while I was dozing off beside the fire on the lapa.

Over time, our encounters with hyenas have provided two of our most memorable experiences.

Dear Dan and Laura,

Just a note to let you know what's happening in the bush.

We had a braai last night. For protection at the braai—and so that I can see if anything is going to attack us—I made a major purchase this year: I bought the world's largest torch. A torch, you recall, is a South African flashlight. This thing is HUGE!!!! It supposedly has eighteen million watts of candlepower. When I shine that sucker into the bush, anything nearby thinks, "Damn, it's daylight already?"

The only problem is that this torch sucks battery power faster than a Times Square billboard. The result is that it lights the bush for only about thirty seconds. After that, it goes dead and the bush becomes dark.

Okay, battery sucking is only one problem. It's also heavy and awkward to carry. It weighs ten to twelve pounds and has a face (i.e., the part with the light) that is easily twenty-four inches in circumference. So let's just say it doesn't win any design awards. Still, it's an awesome torch.

As you can probably tell, I love this thing. Last week when we visited Satara—one of the camps deep in the Kruger—I took along my torch. One of the traditions at Satara is that at night the people gather around a wire fence and look for animals by shining their torches into the bush. Most of these people use tiny little pin lights that meekly search into the darkness. Not me. Children cowered, teenagers asked for autographs, middle-aged men guarded their wives, and old people looked stunned when I walked to the fence with my humongous torch. Everyone wanted to know where I purchased such a marvelous beast. Some even asked if I had to take out a loan to buy it. Grrrrrr!!!! I was the envy of the camp.

Okay, full confession, the admirers mentioned earlier were not overly impressed when the light went out after thirty seconds; but for those thirty seconds I was King of the Camp!

I digress because I just want to emphasize, once again, how much I love my torch.

So this evening we have a braai, and then, as tradition demands, we go into the house to eat what we have prepared. During this time we always leave our cooking utensils outside, along with my torch. (It's too heavy to carry in with anything else. And, truth is, it deserves a proper, honorary exit after each evening's feast.) We have always assumed that everything will be safe since we leave the lanterns lit and the fire on the lapa is still pretty strong.

After we finish eating, I go back outside to gather the utensils, turn off the lanterns, turn on my torch for safety, and head back to the house. The only catch, of course, is that I can't dawdle. I have to get back inside within thirty seconds or even the bush animals will laugh at me.

Well, last night I went outside to collect my belongings and was shocked to discover my torch was missing. I had no idea what happened to it. My only thought was that someone must have wandered by while we were eating and stolen it. That's scary. It means we are much more vulnerable than we thought. It also means we are not alone here. I barely slept last night because of this incident. I was feeling violated and vulnerable.

The actual truth is that I sat up most of the night waiting for someone to burst into the house, shine the torch in my eyes, and say, "This is a Light Up! Give me everything you got." I knew the light would go out quickly, but I still didn't want to have to wrestle with a thieving poacher in the middle of the night. So I was "Sleepless in Sabie Park."

Early this morning, as soon as the sun rose, I went out and again checked the boma for the torch. I thought perhaps I had a little too much wine last night and just didn't see the torch when I went back outside. It would be hard to miss such a large object, but who knows. I once missed downtown Atlanta while driving through it because of a conversation I was having. So perhaps the torch was still there.

But even in the light of early morning, there was no sign of the torch. Depression at the loss of the torch was now accompanied by the fear that follows a sleepless evening in the bush. At least it was daylight.

In an effort to clear my brain, I decided to walk up the driveway and see if I could find any evidence that the thief might have dropped. Well, about fifty meters from the house, deep in the bush, I spotted a piece of black plastic shining in the weeds. Further investigation revealed my torch lying in pieces. The plastic handle is bitten in half, with one of the pieces resting to the side of a thorn tree. The rubber protection that surrounded the face of the torch—remember the large circumference I mentioned earlier?—is now filled with teeth marks. And the entire device is scratched and covered with indentations that indicate it was chewed on.

All the evidence indicates that a hyena took it. He must have put his whole mouth around the torch and dragged it off into the night!!! And, as I mentioned, that sucker is heavy. So he must have carried it all that distance in his mouth. Then, once he felt safe, he munched away at the light until he came to the conclusion that it was not a tasty treat.

Believe it or not, even though the handle is broken off, the front rubber is covered with teeth marks, and the remainder of the torch is scratched and looks pathetic, it still works. What a torch! Mind you, there is no longer a functioning handle, but am I going to look so cool walking around with this twelve-pound device tucked under my arm.

I can't wait for the first South African to ask, "What happened to your torch?"

I'll simply reply, "A hyena ate it." Now that's panache. I can already envision the South African walking away saying, "Now that's a bushman!"

Mind you, I am fully aware of the hypocrisy of being worried about someone stealing my torch and then finding sheer delight in the fact that a hyena had absconded with it. But, for some reason, I feel safer with that knowledge.

More to come later. For now I have to go charge my torch. I hope you folks are well.

Love,
Dad of the Torch

***

Dear Dan and Laura,

Okay, just a quick update as to our goings-on. First, some necessary context. A few nights ago Mom and I had a braai at our house. I later had to call Kim Campbell about some school stuff back in the United States, so I only drank water, no wine. This change in liquid consumption created a very weird evening. Overall, I found the braai terrifying. A stone-sober bush braai leads to the realization that the two of you are sitting alone in the African wilderness with no gun or any other form of protection. This recognition does not induce feelings of security. So by the end of the evening, I vowed never to have a wine-less bush braai again.

Now fast-forward to this evening. Mom and I are having our first braai since the one mentioned above. And, being true to my word, I make sure that I'm fortified before the first log goes onto the fire.

Well, one thing leads to another, and it turns out I'm having a very interesting conversation with a wood owl while cooking our pork chops. The conversation was going well since the wood owl continued to move closer and closer to me. The relationship was getting rather serious, and I was contemplating proposing to the wood owl when I heard Mom say something. I didn't understand what she said since I was deeply involved in this exchange with the wood owl while simultaneously watching those pork chops. Multitasking is necessary even in the bush.

After a few minutes, I felt extreme pressure on my hips. It felt as if someone was grabbing me. I turned, looked, and realized that Mom had walked behind me and seized my hips with both hands. Now, this is a bit unusual. I quickly decided that she must be jealous of the developing wood owl relationship. And based on the firmness with which she was holding my hips, I figured she wanted to reclaim her man with a line dance. Now, a line dance in the bush seems a little kinky, especially with just the two of us being there. I mean, gosh, that train is not going to be very long. But, I figure, "What the heck? So long as the kids don't find out."

So I stand up straight—I had been bending over, adjusting the coals—and get ready to shake my booty. For safety, I figure I better check the surroundings before getting this train in motion. One doesn't want to accidentally walk into the darkness of the bush and trip over a leopard. I therefore divert my attention away from the pork chops, respond with nothing but silence to the hooting of the wood owls, and scan the boma for a path for this train to take. It was only then that I realized why Mom walked behind me. For there, standing smack-dab between the plunge pool and the house—our only route of escape—was a huge, carnivorous-looking hyena.

The firelight reflected straight from hyena's eyes into mine. I looked first at his fiery eyes and then turned and looked directly into Mom's face. In the hyena's eyes I saw fire; in Mom's eyes I saw fear. I turned, looked again at the hyena, and then all three of us looked at the pork chops. The evening's meal was in jeopardy. Perceptively, I realized that Mom didn't want to line dance after all. Nor was she jealous of my conversations with the wood owl. Instead, she had heard the beast coming around the bend and wanted to warn me about it. Well, warn is not exactly the right word. More precisely, I guess you could say, she wanted me, not herself, to be the appetizer to the pork chops. She is always so thoughtful.

Now, on most nights, I would have screamed and run away in terror. I might even have sacrificed your mother in an effort to save my own bones—and those of the pork chops as well. But this evening I was fortified with liquid courage. So instead of wrestling with Mom and trying to throw her to the front of the line, or tossing the pork chops over the fence and shouting "Dinner" to the hyena, I grabbed my torch—the one he ate last month—shined it into his eyes, and shouted, "Get out of here; Get out of here!!!" I even stepped toward him with staggering bravado.

Apparently, the hyena spoke English. Or else he was blinded by my torch. Or, most likely, he was frightened by the fire reflecting off the vast forehead that my receding hairline has left. Who knows? It is difficult to determine what he thought as the light from my torch and the reflections from my forehead grabbed his attention. And remember, I had a torch, twelve lanterns, and a roaring flame reflecting from that receding hairline as well. It must have been one terrifying scene from the hyena's perspective. In any case, it worked. The hyena turned tail and trotted—I wish I could say ran—back into the bush. The pork chops, Mom, and yours truly were all safe and sound. Whew. What a night.

We are now in the television room at the Protea Hotel. Mom is reading and having a milkshake. I'm having another glass of wine and promising that I will never, ever approach another African evening sober.

I hope you guys are well. Mom is driving home tonight.

Love,
Dad of the Shaking Booty

A particularly important and enjoyable aspect of the braai also needs a mention. It is the time in the evening when the burning wood transforms into coal. It is at this moment that a fun ritual takes place.

Shakespeare, Gerard Manley Hopkins, and others were mesmerized by the way a wood fire eventually collapses onto itself. As it did in England in the seventeenth century and Europe in the twentieth century, so it does in South Africa in the twenty-first century: the fire collapses on itself and creates embers—chunks of wood that are extremely hot. These chunks fall into the fire pit of the lapa. During a bush braai, these embers are removed with tongs and transferred to a metal plate. Above this plate is a grill, which is heated by the embers and on which the food cooks.

Most of the food brought outside is cooked on the grill, although some items are placed directly on the hot embers. We particularly enjoy baking potatoes directly on the coals. We wrap the potatoes in tin foil and place them on top of the embers, turning the potato every ten minutes. The potatoes become amazingly tender and tasty in the process. However, taste is not the main reason we like to cook potatoes in this matter. We do so to prolong the braai. In our view, a braai should last as long as possible. Remember, don't forget the setting: we are cooking outside, alone, in the dark, in the African bush. Why would anyone want to rush that experience?

Finally, to fully understand the bush context in which this adventure story takes place, and to cautiously meander a bit further away from the bush house, we need to describe the thrill of traveling on our driveway. This driveway is not just an entrance to a bush house—it is an introduction to the bush as well.

The driveway to Erf 286 is a narrow, two-meter-wide, three-hundred-meter-long dirt path. It twists, turns, and bends between fifty-year-old white-barked marula trees, twisting jackalberry trees, and thorn-filled acacia trees. Supporting the prickly nature of the latter are intermittent protruding thorn bushes along with the craggy roots and sharp, broken trunks of trees pushed out of the ground by elephants. The thorns and scraggly branches of this rugged, thick bush scrape and swipe against any car that meanders down its path. Each scratch of each branch sounds as if it is removing every layer of paint that has ever been on the car. Yet, in thirteen years, we have never found a visible scratch on any of the rental cars we drive. Nor have we ever paid a fine to the rental car companies for such damage.

This protection of the car's exterior comes from nature's built-in speed bumps that protrude along the path. Rocks and boulders that have been in the ground for centuries fill the route. These protrusions severely limit the speed of any cars that seek to travel the route. Generally, cars go no more than one to three kilometers per hour as they proceed along the driveway. These speed restrictions also mean that the trip along the driveway takes between one and a half and two minutes.

It is rather fun to watch cars proceed up and down the driveway. The vehicles shake, bend, and contort as if they are participating in a badly structured carnival ride. Being inside these cars is not so enjoyable. Heads twist, limbs shake, and teeth clatter during the adventure. In fact, you are apt to bite your tongue, literally, if not metaphorically, as the car tips and bumps its way along.

Counterbalancing the harsh scratches on the side of the car is the gentle brush of bush beneath. This bush grows between the two tracks on the path and gently sweeps the under part of the car as it proceeds up and down the driveway.

But there is a reward for traveling the driveway—and the reward is more than just reaching your destination. Stated simply, you never know what the driveway and the nearby bush will show you. Animals feast and sometimes defecate along the path. Kudu, impala, bushbuck, and other forms of antelope frequently appear on the route. Sometimes you have to pause and wait for a zeal of zebra that is walking along or crossing the path. And at least once every two or three weeks, you have to wait while a tower of giraffes munches on those thorn bushes that line the path and scratch against the car.

Giraffes eating from a thorn bush are amazing to watch. Giraffes are browsers, which means they eat vegetation from plants and trees that are above the grass line. They will eat from just about any plant or tree that is located in a safe area, including mimosa, wild apricot, and other fruit-bearing trees. But the acacia is their obvious favorite.

The thorns on the acacia are long, pointed, and extremely sharp. Between the thorns are leaves that giraffes regard as a delicacy. As a result, giraffes have evolved to make this luxury attainable. Sometimes they will use their long tongues to fetch the tasty acacia leaves from between the thorns. I have watched them do this with amazing accuracy. At other times, they will simply grip an entire branch in their mouths and lurch their heads to the side. The result is that the leaves slide off the branch and the giraffes happily munch away on the end product. Both of these approaches are aided by the giraffe's saliva system. Their mouths secrete a heavy, clear fluid with the viscosity of West Texas crude. These fluids protect their mouths from thorn damage. Also, helping this gesture is the fact that giraffes have no teeth in the upper front part of their mouths. Instead, they have a smooth pad that is made slippery through the aforementioned saliva. So when the giraffes pull at the branch, the process is painless and rewarding.

One word of warning about this very efficient system. If you ever hand feed a giraffe, you will quickly discover what this moisture feels like. At best, it feels like a clear, heavy oil. It is not pleasant to touch. If you are ever kissed by a giraffe, well . . . let's just stop with this informative approach and wrap up our trip along the bush house driveway.

The best way to convey what can happen on a trip along the driveway is to describe our single best driveway encounter. On this trip we discovered a visitor we never expected—and haven't seen on our driveway since.

Dear Dan and Laura,

Just a quick note to share an interesting afternoon experience.

We were heading out for lunch at 13:00. As we drove up the driveway, we saw a huge male kudu standing beside a tree. His magnificent horns gave an aura of great command. Usually, male kudus are quiet and dignified. But this one was obviously disturbed. He was loudly barking at something on the other side of the driveway. Whatever it was made him extremely upset.

The kudu did not move as we drove next to him. That is unusual. Generally, kudus walk off with casual dignity if you get too close. But this one let us drive right beside him; we could easily have reached out and touched him. Whatever was bothering him was more important than we were.

Because he was so disturbed, I stopped the car and surveyed where he was looking. His attention was focused on a set of rocks to our right that was about three meters from the car. The rocks are on the side of the driveway opposite from where the kudu was standing.

We looked and looked but couldn't see anything other than rocks and thorny scrub bush. Then, suddenly, the head of a huge leopard appeared from behind the rocks. He apparently had been sleeping on one of the back rocks. I make that observation based on the fact that he gave out two big yawns. My guess is that the kudu's barking, combined with the noise from the engine of the car, probably woke him.

The leopard was magnificent. His face had the rosette pattern that defines the species. The patterns on his face were small, especially in comparison to his head, which was huge. Based on this size we quickly estimated that he was a mature male, probably about fifteen years old.

Once the leopard raised his head, the kudu became quiet.

After the leopard completed his second yawn, he stared directly at the kudu. Not too surprisingly, the magnificent male kudu scampered off into the bush like a bespeckled first-grader running from a sixth-grade bully. "Better to live to bark another day" seemed to be this kudu's mantra.

That left Mom and me, sitting alone in the car, as the only living creatures in the area. The leopard turned his head and promptly focused his stare on us. He looked at us for about thirty seconds. Then he looked away, yawned again, and quickly refocused his stare back on us.

The leopard's look was intimidating. It was as if he were saying, "What in the hell are you doing here?" However, while intimidating, the look was not threatening. He seemed to be studying us more than wanting to scare us. It was as if he was trying to figure us out while simultaneously dominating us. Realistically, we had little risk since we were in the car with the windows and doors closed. I'm still learning about bush life, but I think it is a safe conclusion that leopards don't know how to open a car door. Just in case, though, we locked the doors.

This second look from the leopard lasted for two minutes. We stared back in amazement. Finally, he decided it was time to expand the experience. So he climbed to the top of the rock to give us a full view of his body. His body was proportional to his head. In other words, he was huge!!! Did I mention that already? He was easily two and a half feet high—a height that seemed even taller since the rocks he was standing on were above us. He must have weighed between 175 and 200 pounds.

Once he got to the top of the rocks, he looked away, stretched three times to show us his muscles and limberness, and then began slowly walking over the rocks directly toward the car. We checked the locks and the windows. He wasn't rushing. He was just casually walking toward us.

When he got a meter away, he paused, looked directly at us, and then turned and walked toward the back of the car. Once there he glanced back toward the car, stepped onto the driveway, and headed toward our house.

At this point Mom shouted, "Follow him! Follow him!" I

agreed with the intention but had the challenge of turning around the car in the narrow driveway. We were pointed "up" the driveway while he was going "down."

Desperate times call for desperate measures. I drove the car into the bush, backed up across the driveway, and proceeded to back firmly into a marula tree. I then drove forward into the bush, narrowly avoided hitting another tree, and then backed up with the intention of getting centered on the driveway. Sadly, the best of intentions often go astray. In short, I backed into the marula tree again. There are now two large dents on the bumper and the trunk of the rental car. I did, however, manage to get the car turned around after the second bump. The good news was that the leopard wasn't watching. It would have been embarrassing.

We caught up with the leopard about ten meters down the driveway. He was in no rush. We followed him as he walked slowly down the remainder of the driveway. He turned once and acknowledged us, but he didn't seem disturbed by our desire to see more. In fact, he seemed to enjoy the attention—or, should I say, "adulation." He carried himself with a confidence that said, "I own this bush." Eventually, he arrived at the house, paused, and surveyed the carport. He was obviously familiar with the area. He looked into the carport for thirty seconds and saw nothing of interest. So he turned to us, gave an expression that said, "I have seen enough of the two of you," and darted into the bush. He disappeared instantly. Gone. Vanished.

What an experience! You realize I walk up and down that driveway every morning for exercise? I'll walk a little more carefully in the future. Perhaps I'll ride instead. It's also disturbing to realize how visible he was at one moment and how invisible he became at the next. It makes one wonder what else is in that bush. Perhaps what you think is there and what is there may not always be the same.

By the way, don't plan on a big inheritance. Repairing those dents in the bumper and trunk is going to be expensive. But no matter the price, the experience was worth it! If necessary, you can recoup some of the money by putting us in a lower-cost nursing home. We won't know the difference. We will be talking about leopards in our driveway, and the nursing staff will simply nod and say to one another, "Wow, leopards in their driveway. These two have really lost it. I hear they used to be lucid."

I hope you folks are well.

Love,
Your NASCAR Dad

Sabie Park, the bush house, the braai, and even the driveway—each location provides context for the story of our African adventure. They also provide the setting in which our quest to approach an elephant is about to take place. Each location will additionally play important roles within this story as it unfolds.

CHAPTER SEVEN

Take a Walk on the Wild Side

Courage is being scared to death . . .
and saddling up anyway.
—John Wayne

Chapter 7

The quest to approach a wild African elephant continued with limited success over a number of winter visits. Some years no elephants came close enough to the fence for me to practice an approach. On other occasions, when an elephant did step forward, I became frightened, turned tail, and scooted away as soon as the elephant began its mock charge.

Slowly, however, a slight change began to develop. It is inappropriate to say I conquered fear. It may be more accurate to say I became comfortable living with it. Courage and fear have a symbiotic relationship. To be courageous one must also be fearful. Courage without fear is just action.

The first glimmer of hope that I would ever successfully approach an elephant came at the beginning of our seventh winter living in Africa.

Dear Dan and Laura,

We are off to a good start this year. We have been here three days and already a small herd of elephants—eight in all—has come into the backyard twice. So we're making progress. And speaking of progress, let me briefly share the latest development in my quest to approach an elephant.

The aforementioned herd of eight elephants showed up yesterday afternoon while Mom and I were having coffee on the back stoep. The herd had two "youngish" elephants (I'd estimate their age as three years old), three adolescent elephants, and three fully developed, mature elephants.

The herd approached with its normal announcement: the crackle of breaking reeds and broken tree branches. Each elephant moved quickly into the backyard and then dispersed about the area. One of the mature elephants went alone beneath the large jackalberry tree that sits to the left of our house on the Kruger side of the fence. She was in an open area beneath the tree.

I couldn't resist; I had to get closer. Mom agreed that it was a good opportunity to do so. She also said, "I'll the keep the door open just in case." Mom additionally reminded me not to stray too far from the full-grown trees on our side of the fence. There are useful to hide behind in the event that problems develop during the approach.

I walked away from the house, parallel to the wire fence that was separating the elephant and me. The fence was five meters away. The elephant was standing ten meters on the other side of the fence. My intention was to get toward the front of the elephant so as not to surprise it from the side.

Once I got into position, I lowered my head, evoked humbling thoughts about the elephant's stature compared with mine, and started to move slowly toward the fence. I got within one meter of the fence but couldn't stand the temptation. I had to look up. When I did, I saw the elephant staring at me with its ears set wide apart. I was making progress. The elephant's eyes, which I could see clearly, projected an air of kindness mixed with concern about my intentions.

Shortly after I looked up, the elephant took two steps toward me and paused. She didn't trumpet nor could the movement in any way be labeled a mock charge. She wasn't going that fast. Also, her trunk was still hanging loosely from her head.

Now for purposes of full disclosure—and since later versions of this story will probably claim otherwise—I acknowledge that I backed up two steps as soon as she started toward me. I resumed my humble stance by looking down. I heard some movement after that, but it didn't seem rushed, so I remained in place. When I next looked up, the elephant was five meters in front of me. She was staring intently with her ears fully extended. Her look, as far as I could interpret, seemed to have changed from a mixture of kindness and concern to one of perturbation that I was present. At this point, we were on the edge of crossing into each other's space. I also realized that my escape path was getting limited in the event that she charged. There was no longer enough space to turn and hustle toward those solid trees. So I decided to leave.

Slowly, with my head still down in a humble position, I turned away from the elephant and began walking parallel to the fence in the direction of the house. It didn't occur to me when I started, but I was walking into an open area that was further away from the protection of the trees.

I was stunned by the elephant's reaction. She turned and followed me as I walked away. At first I could hear her walking along, and then I glanced back and saw her moving with me. It was amazing! There I was walking parallel to our fence with an elephant following in the same direction. It looked like a man going for a walk with his pet dog. Only this dog weighed three tons and was a wild African elephant. She remained about five meters to my side and one meter behind me as we walked. It would have been wonderful if Mom had had a camera. It would have been a picture to treasure forever. I'll just have to remember it through this email. The exhilaration of the moment was palpable.

We proceeded in this direction for about ten meters. Then, the elephant turned left and headed back into the Kruger. The other elephants had, by this point, gone back into the Kruger. She was simply returning to her herd.

I walked to the house and expected Mom to extol my courage. Her husband had to have proven himself more courageous than she ever thought. The approach was not exactly successful, but it was getting closer. Also, I arrogantly thought Mom would be impressed by what I had accomplished. Wrong!

Her first words were a question: "Are you stupid?" Before I had a chance to answer, she observed that I had foolishly walked away from my tree coverage.

"What if that elephant had come after you?" she added. "You're not that fast. You could not have gotten away."

Then, before I could defend myself, she turned and walked into the house, closing the door behind her. She added one last observation before the door went shut: "Just make sure you keep the life insurance fully paid."

Overall, not the reaction I anticipated.

I hope you guys are well. Let me know if Mom inquires about a divorce attorney.

Love,
Dad, the Elephant Walker

Even though Sally was upset that my foray with the elephant had become a little too dangerous, the marriage itself was not in jeopardy. The previous summer we had celebrated our fortieth wedding anniversary while staying at the bush house. On that day we flew to Zimbabwe to see Victoria Falls. The night before, however, the bush offered a marriage-testing experience that proved that while fear needs to be present for courage to prove itself, humility and laughter are virtues as well. All in all, the experience was not my finest moment.

Dear Dan and Laura,

Just a quick update about what happened last night after Mom and I talked with both of you. By the way, we leave for Harare, Zimbabwe, in an hour so this note is written in haste.

This year Mom and I have developed a new evening ritual—feeding bananas to bush babies. These animals are amazing. They are part of the monkey family but have faces that look like tiny cats, including the same pointy ears as cats. Every night when we start the braai, we cut up two or three bananas and place them on a nearby table. Then, pretty soon, two or three bush babies appear and feast heartily on each piece of banana.

A couple of amazing facts about bush babies. First, they are extremely proficient climbers. They secrete a fluid through their genitalia that is sticky. They rub their paws against the genitalia to ensure stickiness. Once they have this stuff on their paws, they can go just about anywhere. Ours often climb up and down the bricks on the side of the house. It's rather amazing how they stick to the side of the house even though they are not small animals. They probably weigh between three and four kilos. I wish my genitalia were that useful.

Bush babies have one fatal flaw: bananas. They cannot resist them. To make their lives extremely complicated, their paws are built in such a way that they have extreme difficulty peeling a banana. Hence, when they see or smell a peeled banana, they just have to come get it. The result is that they are willing to venture close to humans to gather the treat.

On most nights we place the bananas on a table when we start the braai. The table is about five meters from us. But last night we ate at the Protea so that we could call you. Hence, we didn't have a braai. But when we got home, we decided to try a little experiment. We wanted to see how close the bush babies would come in order to get the bananas. So we placed the peeled bananas on a table on the back stoep and moved the table right beside the sliding-glass door that goes into the house. Then, we turned on the light that is over the stoep and turned off all the other lights in the house. Finally, we opened the sliding door and screen that go out to the stoep and placed two chairs right beside the entrance. There we sat and waited. If the bush babies wanted those bananas, they would have to come less than a meter away from us to collect the feast.

So here is the picture: two elderly people sitting in the dark beside an open sliding door in the African bush. Outside is a well-lit table with peeled bananas sitting on it. To make matters more interesting, it is the eve of this couple's fortieth wedding anniversary. Who would have thought that they would end up here after forty years?

The night was cold, and a stiff wind was blowing from the Kruger. I pulled a white duvet from the nearby bedroom to cover Mom and me as we waited for the bush babies to appear.

The bush, by the way, was pitch black. This darkness contrasted sharply with the light from the stoep. Stated simply, the bush looked ominous.

We sat in the doorway for fifteen minutes. No bush babies appeared. In fact, nothing came past. Eventually, Mom asked an intriguing question: "What if something else tries to get in here?"

She pointed out that we couldn't see anything beyond the light on the back stoep. So, she asked, what will we do if a leopard, a hyena, or perhaps even a lion suddenly appears?

I had been pondering the same question since we sat down. But once Mom raised the topic, my protective male instincts kicked in. I didn't want my bush mate feeling frightened. She was safe with me. So I replied with confidence, "Not to worry; even at sixty-four, I still have cat-like instincts. You will be astounded at the speed and agility I'll demonstrate closing that door if a leopard or a hyena tries to get in here. You won't even have moved by the time I've closed the sliding window, locked it, and sat back down on the couch."

Mom seemed satisfied. Confidence is king in the world of the bush!

By now it was 10:00 p.m.—well beyond my bedtime. Additionally, as you might have guessed, I had earlier consumed two well-filled glasses of wine at the Protea. This combination of being bone-tired and in a liquid haze led me to doze off a bit—although I am certain my cat-like instincts were still intact.

We sat for another ten minutes after this conversation. All the while I was nodding off and popping back awake. Then, suddenly, during one of my moments of alertness, the most awesome bat/bird/eagle or whatever it was came flying from the bush toward the house. It came straight toward the open door. The beast was pure white and huge. Its wingspan was easily two meters. At first I thought I was dreaming, but then I realized I was awake!

My response? I jumped up from the chair like a frightened child and began screaming "no, no, no!" Even worse, at the same time that I was screaming, I picked up the duvet and pulled it over my head. Mom and I disagree somewhat on this matter. I contend that I was trying to make sure we were both covered. But Mom points out that I was the only one covered. If time had not been of the essence, I would have covered her next.

In any case, the next steps are not debatable. My scary movie/roller-coaster screams worked. The beast flew toward us and swooped onto the stoep, but then did a 180-degree turn and flew back into the Kruger. It might have helped that I was still standing in the doorway, covered with a white duvet, shouting "no, no, no!" I looked like a ghost.

Again, from my viewpoint, the strategy was effective. The beast flew away. When it did so, Mom stood up, closed the sliding door, and muttered softly, but with loving sarcasm dripping from her lips, "My hero."

As calm returned, we both sat down. I looked at Mom and said, "Boy, you are lucky I was here to protect you."

She looked at me seriously for a moment, and then we both burst into huge rounds of laughter. You never know how you will respond in a crisis until you face one. In this instance, I humbly submit that I was not the hero.

In case you're wondering, the bush babies never showed up. My screams probably sent them halfway to Mozambique.

I hope you guys are well.

Love,
Dad, Your Hero

In my defense, it seems reasonable to scream in fright at the sight of a huge winged animal flying toward you from the bush at 10:10 p.m. That's a scary situation. And since fear is a necessary ingredient of courage, screaming is oral proof that an ample dosage of fear was present. Furthermore, people who are only fearful won't go back to the root cause of the fear. We did. Within a week, my wife and I were back sitting in the dark, watching bush babies eat bananas on our back stoep. The door, however, was closed. Courage doesn't mean you foolishly repeat your mistakes.

CHAPTER EIGHT

When I Have Fears

When I have fears that I may cease to be . . .
—John Keats

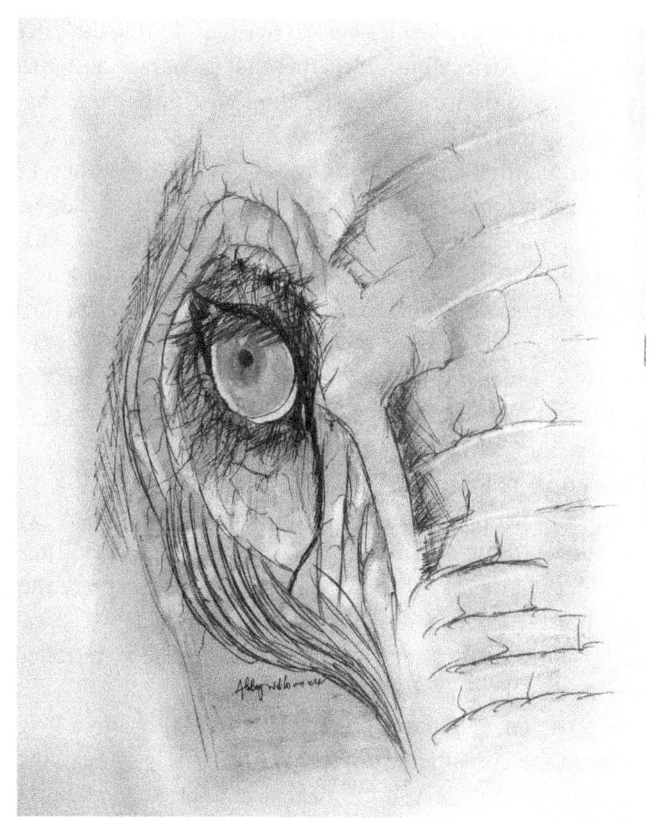

People often ask if we are ever afraid while living in the African bush. The honest answer is, "Yes—constantly." The glib answer that always gets a chuckle but might be even truer is, "No, we're never afraid. Terrified, yes . . . afraid? Never."

At the outset, let me also add that I initially abandoned this entire chapter. It is adventurous but so filled with risks that any rational person would ask, "Why go live in the African bush?" Additionally, this chapter describes events that never get resolved. Hence, the sources of the fear are still out there. In fact, if anything, the dangers may be greater today than they were a decade ago. Poaching is far worse now than it was when we first moved to South Africa.

Fear is a constant in the African bush. And full disclosure, I doubt we would continue to live in the African bush if our children were young and dependent on us. The risk is just too great. So we haven't overcome fear; we have just learned to live with it. It is the price you pay to live in the African bush. Whether that is courage or not we will leave for others to decide. However, I think that by living in the bush we are proving that fear can be lived with.

Fear is at its worst around 3:00 a.m. It is at this time when I occasionally wake up, shake the mental cobwebs from my head, and realize where we are living. The house at this point is totally dark. The bush is usually silent. I lie awake in this setting wondering what I will do if a light appears outside the house. Or, even worse, will my heart be able to withstand a knock on the door? Our only protection is a walking stick, which I keep beside the bed, and a small hatchet that is used to clear bush. Neither will provide much protection against a nighttime visitor carrying a gun built to kill rhinos.

Considering its location, Sabie Park is relatively safe. The park is separated from the outside area by a four-meter electrified fence that surrounds everything but the area that abuts the Kruger. The environment that surrounds Sabie Park is remote bush except for the Protea Hotel nearby. The nearest community, Mukhulu, is fifteen kilometers away. Additionally, the entrance to Sabie Park is controlled and manned around the clock by a guard.

The electric fence that surrounds Sabie Park drops to a height of one meter in the areas that touch the Kruger. Until this year, the bottom of the fence has been open so that animals such as bushbuck, guinea fowl, and impala can scoot beneath. Other animals, such as kudu and leopards, simply leap over the fence.

It is probably apparent by now that our fears focus not on wild animals. Lions, leopards, hyena, baboons—these can be dealt with. We can control the level of risk that we take with these animals. We know that an encounter is possible when we go outside. At the same time, we also know that we can seek shelter and safety in the bush house should the danger become too great. So it is not the animals about which we worry—it is the people. This is a risk over which we have less control.

It is impossible to ignore the poverty of South Africa. It is endemic. Conditions are often deplorable. Almost 22 percent of the people in South Africa live in what is labeled "extreme poverty." This designation means they are not able to pay for basic nutritional requirements. An additional 15 percent of the people are unable to pay for food and nonfood items. Hence, they sacrifice food for other necessities such as transport. Finally, 53.8 percent of the population can afford food and nonfood items but fall under the broad definition of poverty—that is, they survive with an income of less than R779 ($52.00) a month.

To bring the matter closer to home, here are statistics for Mpumalanga, the province in which Sabie Park and the Kruger are located. Almost 20 percent of the population lives in government-subsidized dwellings. Twenty-nine percent of the population has access to piped water in their main dwelling, while 44.4 percent has access to piped water in the yard. An additional 5.4 percent of the population has access to piped water that is no more than two kilometers from the main dwelling. Finally, and most strikingly, 22.7 percent has no access to safe drinking water.

Living conditions such as these make for neither a pleasant nor a healthy lifestyle. If I were existing—living might be too kind a word—in these conditions, and if I saw what I perceived as "wealthy" outsiders occupying a house on my native country's land, I would be sorely tempted to seek some portion of their goods. Hence, stealing is a problem. And while our bush house has not been broken into so far, other houses in Sabie Park have been robbed. Thus far, the break-ins have occurred only when the houses were empty. But it is only a matter of time until an accidental encounter occurs between a would-be thief and an occupant. We will see what happens then.

A more immediate safety concern is the fence that separates our yard from the Kruger. While the fence controls access to most animals, it provides little barrier to enterprising burglars. It would be relatively simple for someone to navigate through the fence. Plus, there is almost no fence a few hundred meters from our house where a community park is located. Of course to get to these areas the assailants would have to walk through the Kruger's wilderness and ford the Sabie river. Thus, ironically, crocodiles and lions provide a safety net from would-be break-ins. Plus, there are those hippos in the river, and they kill more people than . . . you get the point.

Yet the fence creates a point of vulnerability, especially considering the isolated area in which we live. The risk comes from poachers. Here is a group of individuals who work in an environment that contains lions, crocodiles, and hippos. Rhino poachers are the specific subset of poachers that create the most worry for us.

Kruger is a rhino poacher's paradise. In 2015, the continent of Africa contained approximately 25,000 rhinos. Of these, more than 8,400 were located in the Kruger. Hence, just as Willie Sutton robbed banks because that is where the money is, so rhino poachers come to the Kruger because that is where the rhinos are.

Poachers have decimated the rhino population in Kruger Park over the past decade. A total of 1,215 rhinoceroses were poached in 2014, with 386 suspected poachers arrested. In 2015, an additional 1,175 rhinoceroses were killed, with 318 suspected poachers arrested. Needless to say, even though the number of rhinos killed decreased slightly, the overall trend is alarming. Extinction is a possibility, if not a probability.

The section of Kruger our bush house abuts is rhino country. We see one or more rhinos at least once a week during our afternoon drives. On rare occasions rhinos have even shown up at the fence in our backyard. And while it is frightening to acknowledge, we have to confess that on occasion we hear gunshots in the middle of the night. We never know if the shots come from guards scaring off poachers or poachers taking the lives of an unsuspecting rhino. We do, however, sometimes learn the results of the gunshots—another rhino is gone. That truly is tragic.

The South African government and Kruger authorities are working diligently to get control of this problem. Evidence of these efforts surrounds us. Heavily armed guards pass beside Sabie Park and enter the Kruger at least once a week. Truckloads of military personnel riding in armored vehicles enter the park through the Paul Kruger Gate every week or two. It is pleasing to see that the national government and park authorities taking dramatic action to control this problem; yet, at the same time, it is a bit unsettling knowing that guards and poachers might be having an exchange of gunfire "in the neighborhood." No reasonable person wants to live in a war zone.

On a personal level, it is impossible to calculate the actual risk of being harmed by poachers. On the one hand, poachers kill animals, not people. Their intention is to remove the horn from a rhino, usually by killing the rhino first, and then to profit from the sale of the horn. Poachers do not enter the bush intending to hurt or rob two Americans sitting alone in a bush house.

On the other hand, we might prove tempting bait. We are an easy mark sitting unprotected in the bush. Although we keep no valuables in the house, and just enough money to live on, the poachers don't know that. So while they may enter the park planning to kill a rhino—for which, by the way, there is more financial incentive than there is in robbing two elderly Americans—poachers could accidentally stumble upon us and decide that a little chump change might be easy pickings. If that ever happens, then we become the chumps.

Our single most frightening incident occurred in the midst of a braai. Poachers may or may not have been involved. We never found out. Even a cursory review of this email brings back chilling thoughts of an evening that may have been scripted by Alfred Hitchcock.

Greetings Dan and Laura,

All is well. I just wanted to record another facet of this year's trip. Feel free to skip this email should you have better things to do—but it might be worth reading in the event that we're never heard from again.

We decided to have a braai last night. Nothing unusual about that. I lit the lanterns and started the fire while Mom put out bananas for bush babies. We haven't seen the bush babies for a while; they may have found a different set of banana pigeons.

Much to our surprise, a severe windstorm kicked up as soon as the fire and lanterns were lit. Storms such as these are unusual at this time of year. This storm was the first ever to occur during a braai.

The wind whistled through the trees and bent the branches with amazing ease. The lanterns hanging on the cane fence were swinging like a railroad man directing traffic in the dark.

The fire in one of the lanterns got so stoked that it leaped out of the top and began burning the cane fence on which the lantern was hanging. I doused the flames with bottled water. No major damage to the fence, but a nasty plume of smoke emerged.

The fire on the lapa, meanwhile, began sending a plethora of sparks and embers into the trees and the nearby bush. The sparks were flying right over the cane fence. Needless to say, this quickly became an emergency situation since the bush is dry this time of year.

Thoughts of starting a bush fire ran through both of our minds—as well as fear of lighting the house itself on fire. That thatch roof is flammable. So after a brief assessment of the situation, we halted the braai and went into safety mode. We doused the fire with buckets of water and turned off the lanterns. Within a few minutes there was lots of smoke but no active flames.

It was now almost 19:00—too late to use our private dining area at the Protea. It was also an extremely dark and spooky night since the wind was still blowing crazily and clouds were covering the stars and the moon. Rather than leave the bush house, we decided to have a "patched dinner" of leftover pork chops and hot dogs. To add a little bush flavor to the meal, and since the weather was so intriguing, we decided to eat outside on the back stoep. A secondary reason for sitting there was so we could respond quickly just in case we discovered some embers were still burning. Even a minor fire mistake in these conditions would be disastrous.

So we set up shop and ate beside the bush baby's bananas on the back veranda. The scene was dramatic. The wind was rushing out of the bush with amazing force. Tree branches were creaking and the trees themselves seemed to be moaning. But we felt safe and cozy on the back stoep. Apparently, a major weather change, a cold front, was moving into the area.

Now, a strange but relevant aside. We recently read a book entitled *The Elephant Whisperer*. I highly recommend it. The book is set in South Africa and deals with an elephant herd that previously lived not too far from here. The herd was moved to a private reserve in KwaZulu-Natal after it began causing too much trouble in this area. The owner's charge was to get the elephants under control.

Two years ago, Mom and I stayed in a national park that was close to where the elephants were moved and where the majority of the book's action takes place. Neither of us had read the book at this time, so we didn't recognize the importance of where we were. That's a description for much of life—both in Africa and the United States.

A very dramatic part of *The Elephant Whisperer* deals with poaching. The authors talk about the ruthlessness of poachers and describe an exchange of gunfire they had with these people. Stated simply, poachers, like drug dealers, are "mean and nasty people."

At present, the rhino poaching here is worse than ever. Two weeks ago, eight rhinos were killed in Kruger in one night.

In *The Elephant Whisperer*, the author describes a technique that poachers use to travel undetected through the bush at night. The technique involves poachers turning their flashlights on and off while they walk through the bush. The poachers need light to see where they are going and to avoid tripping or stepping on snakes or other wild animals. At the same time, they need the cover of darkness to avoid being detected by local authorities. Hence, they flick their lights on and off as they travel through the bush.

Now, I have always assumed that we are relatively safe from poachers since they would have to cross the Sabie River to get to us. We have nothing they want. But still, we are cautious and aware of the risk. And, truth is, even though the river has crocodiles, it also has lots of rocks to step on, and the water is not very deep. So it's crossable.

Back to our feast of hot dogs and cold pork chops. The meal was tasty and the setting dramatic. The wind continued to howl and various parts of the house began to make noises similar to those an old person makes when moving. The joints of the house creaked, groaned, and moaned as the wind shifted the bones of a house that had not been moved for years. It was a great atmosphere.

We were approaching the end of the meal and contemplating what we could find for dessert when Mom suddenly jumped up from her chair and said, "I just saw a light in the bush."

"Yikes!" I thought to myself, but I knew that I had to respond with composure. So with pseudo confidence, I replied, "No way."

She continued to insist that she had seen a light. I continued to contend that her imagination was running wild. I have to confess, though, that while I was questioning her vision, I was simultaneously scanning the bush, looking for evidence of what she had seen. I saw nothing but was frightened anyway.

The debate about the validity of Mom's vision didn't last long. We decided to seek the safest course of action possible. We got up, picked up our dirty plates, hustled into the house, and locked the doors. "Dinner was over anyway," I proclaimed with an air of certainty while checking to make sure the doors were locked. "And we don't need dessert," I added.

Now here is where things get really weird and worthy of Hitchcock. As soon as we got inside the house, the lights went off. My heart jumped into my throat. It was totally dark. I was scared out of my wits. My actual thoughts were, "If this were a movie, it would be really scary." Unfortunately, it was not a movie.

I scrambled about in the dark and found a torch (i.e., a flashlight) inside the pocket of my jacket. We used the light from that torch to find another one. Once we had two torches lit, we went to the window and started shining them outside. There was nothing to see except our lights shining in the dark.

I decided to check the other side of the house and went into the side bedroom and started shining the light onto that side of the bush. That's when Mom, who had turned off her torch, shouted, "There is a light shining on our house! It's on this window!" I came running back, but by the time I got to her side of the house, the light was gone. Mom was shaking with fear. To console her, I came up with the explanation that it was probably just a reflection from the light that I was shining from the other side. I didn't believe that and neither did she. The strength of this argument got undercut even further when I went back into the bedroom and tried to make the light shine on the other side of the house. It didn't work.

Now, at this point we faced some interesting strategic choices. One option, the Charm-the-Potential-Poachers approach, involved me taking my torch, walking outside to the fence, and asking the "light shiners" if they needed help. This option would certainly surprise the poachers, but if it didn't work, the consequences could be severe.

A second option was the Huddle-and-Hope option. This choice involved staying behind the locked doors, closing the window curtains, and huddling in dark silence, hoping the "light shiners" would go away.

As we pondered these options, another strange event occurred: suddenly, the house lights came back on. Remember, we're on a solar system, so this has to be our system going crazy—it's not a power company problem. I'm not exactly sure why, and I guarantee you it was not bravery, but the return of the lights re-invigorated my courage, so I went outside to check on the solar system. I thought perhaps the wind had shaken the cables loose. The solar system is on the side of the house opposite the Kruger, so I was going in the direction opposite from where the light had come.

The solar system looked fine. The connecting cables are underground, so the wind didn't affect them. This also meant that the cables were not cut—which was a relief. The solar panels sit on a pole, so there is a good chance that the wind shaking the pole caused the system to shut down. The panels were still shaking since the wind was still blowing strongly. This quick review led to the conclusion that the lights in the bush and the solar-system shut down were unrelated.

Mom stayed locked in the house during this analysis. And remember, the solar panels are on the side of the house opposite from the bush. But I couldn't resist taking a peek. So I turned off my torch, edged to the side of the house, and gazed around the corner. From here, I was looking directly at the Kruger. At first, I couldn't see anything in the total darkness. Soon, though, I saw blinking lights in the bush. They seemed to be moving away from us, although that might have been wishful thinking. They were not, I determined, moving toward us. Of that I was certain.

The movement of the light away from the house quelled my fears a bit. Still, I was "massively frightened." And I realized there was no guarantee that the light holders wouldn't turn around and come back.

So as I was standing alone outside in the wind, I began again reviewing our safety options. The now revised Let's-Have-a-Late-Evening-Chat-at-the-Fence choice still had little appeal. One might just as well invite the poachers in for tea if we chose that option. However, the Huddle-and-Hope selection had an equally low level of appeal. There was no reason to believe that poachers would respond with empathy if they found two old Americans fearfully huddled together inside a house. I doubt the poachers would feel sympathy, hand us one of their rhino-killing guns, and say, "Here, don't leave yourselves so vulnerable next time."

After dismissing these two options, I developed a third, more appealing alternative. The initial title for this approach was "Run Like a Coward." However, by the time I had entered the house, I had framed it with a more appropriate label. I called it "A Dignified Retreat." So as soon as I found Mom, I proposed that we head to the Protea for dessert. I confessed that I, too, had now seen the lights, but added that they seemed to be moving away from us. Mom shared my concern that the bearers of the lights could return. So, for safety's sake, we agreed to leave. The visitors could take whatever they wanted from the house—except us. And if we weren't there, they could not take that.

So head to the Protea we did. We watched television for

four hours. Mom downed two milkshakes, and I had multiple glasses of wine. (Don't worry. If I ever get killed, I won't go down sober. If nothing else, this should reduce embalming costs. If necessary, just tell the undertaker I was already pickled.)

By the time we left the Protea it was raining really hard—that's the first time that has happened. We stopped at the Sabie Park guard gate to report what had happened earlier. Strangely, we didn't tell the guard when we left. I guess it's male pride or something. I didn't want to report when we were running away, but I was more than willing to say, "We're going back in." There must still be a kernel of pride left in me.

We got back to the house safely and found no evidence that anyone had been in or had even tried to get into the house. Most likely the light shiners saw the house, figured that people were staying there, and then headed back into the bush to do whatever you do in the bush on a windy, rainy night. Our hope was that they found a dry place elsewhere. Luckily, they didn't seek shelter with us.

Needless to say, we did not get what one would label a "good night's rest" last night. Every time a hippo grunted or a bush baby screeched, I was out of bed, stick in hand, ready to take on whoever entered. A nap may be in the offing later today.

That's all for now. We will keep you informed as to the adventures of the Poacher Pushers.

I hope you folks are well.

Love,
Dad, the Terrified

PS: Lest you think we returned to the house out of courage—fearing nothing—that's not true. We checked to see if a room was available at the Protea. Unfortunately, the hotel was fully booked. Also, I had the staff check for hotels in Hazyview. Again, everything was booked. It's the "high tourist" season here. So we returned to the bush house because the only other sleeping option was in the car in the hotel parking lot. And, I must confess, we seriously pondered that option.

We never learned the source of the lights. It might have been guards looking for poachers, it might have been poachers looking for rhinos, or perhaps it was just a few Polish Americans looking for mushrooms. We never found out.

CHAPTER NINE

Fears and Foolishness

The fool doth think he is wise, but the wise man knows himself to be a fool.
—William Shakespeare

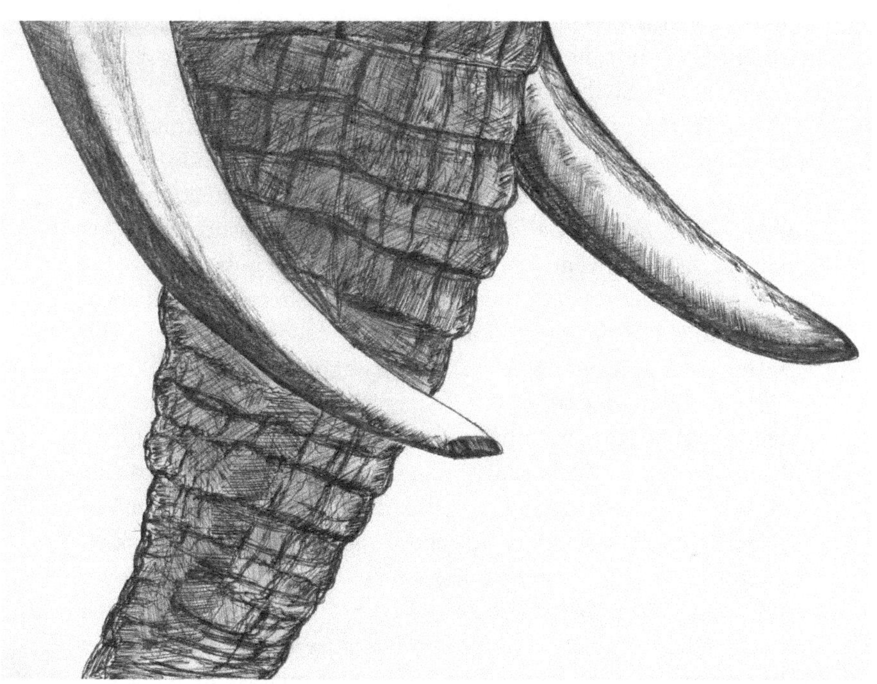

The level of fear we have while living in the bush has been a surprise. I expected to be somewhat frightened when we first moved here. But I assumed that over time I would adjust to the situation and become less fearful. So far that has not happened. To my surprise, I was initially much more terrified than I expected to be. And to my further surprise, time has not reduced that fear. In short, I find myself cautious and a bit frightened every year when we arrive in Johannesburg. It is almost as if I re-remember the multiple risks and am therefore more scared than ever. Sometimes knowledge can be frightening.

Over the years I have taken various steps to lessen the fear. Two, in particular, deserve mention. The first involved buying a gun; the second involved purchasing a can of Mace. Each action deserves an explanation. Further, each action shows that fear can have a lighter side. To say that I laugh in the face of fear is fictitious. To say that fear makes me do laughable things is precisely on target.

My first attempt to feel safer in the African bush involved the purchase of a gun. Gun laws in South Africa are stringent. It is almost impossible for a foreigner to buy a gun legally. Additionally, I do not own nor do I know how to use a weapon. It is, however, possible to buy a paint gun. So that's what I did.

I bought the paint gun shortly after we arrived in Johannesburg, and by the time we drove to Sabie Park, I realized how idiotic the purchase was. I do not know what I was thinking. If my intentions were to bluff a poacher, then a paint gun wasn't going to work. It doesn't even look like a conventional gun. If my intentions were to shoot the poacher with a paint pellet, then the only avenue to safety was that the poacher might die laughing. Sometimes fear can be humbling. I still have the paint gun, but I've never taken it out of its box.

My second attempt at bush safety involved a decision that was a bit more rational: I bought a can of Mace. The thought was that if an intruder broke into the house, I could spray him with the ingredients and Sally and I could scramble to the car and escape. I kept the can of Mace on the bed stand for one entire winter's visit. I even took off the protective cap. I wanted no delays if anyone entered the bedroom without invitation. Unfortunately, as I eventually learned, just as one should exercise special caution when handling a loaded weapon, so likewise one should be especially careful with a topless can of Mace.

I found the can of Mace still sitting on the bed stand when we returned the next year. It was still primed and ready to go. Even the protective cap was still sitting to the side.

The next day, our second day of this year's visit, we drove to Hazyview, the nearest city of significant size, to buy supplies and other essentials. The drive to Hazyview takes forty-five minutes. It entails going through some very impoverished sections of South Africa.

Hazyview is a beehive of activity far different from any city in the United States. People are everywhere. They walk along the highways and streets, hang out in groups beside the mall, and wait in long lines to use outside ATMs. Along the street you can buy bedspreads, wood, fresh fish, woodcarvings, oranges, avocados, and an assortment of other goods.

Additionally, carjacking is always a risk in South Africa. Thirty cars a day on average are hijacked in South Africa. Signs along major highways identify high-risk carjacking sites. It is a bit discomforting to read a sign warning you to be cautious of carjacking as you drive through the area where the carjacking occurs.

All things considered, it seemed like a good idea to bring along the can of Mace for the season's first trip to Hazyview. I therefore removed the canister from the bed stand and placed it into my pants pocket. The Mace was loaded and ready to shoot.

Dear Dan and Laura,

We did a supply run to Hazyview earlier today. To get there we have to drive through an area called Bushbuckridge, one of the poorest and most dangerous communities in all of South Africa. Hazyview itself is no haven of safety either, as evidenced by a recent midday bank robbery that included shots being fired at the Blue Haze Mall. So, for protection, I found a can of Mace that I had bought last year and stuck it in the pocket of my jeans.

Did I mention that the Mace can was loaded and ready to shoot?

So we're driving through the city of Mukhulu, which is the halfway point between Sabie Park and Hazyview and is in one of the major towns in Bushbuckridge. There is a lot of traffic, and I'm struggling a bit with the rental car. It is a stick shift, and it is taking me a while to get used to the clutch. And, of course, I am adjusting to driving on the left rather than the right side of the road.

Suddenly, as happens often in South Africa, one car comes shooting past me on the right while another is coming toward us while passing another car. To be clear, the passing car is coming toward us in our driving lane. Then, out of nowhere, a third car pulls in front of us from a side road. At this point, in a panic, I rapidly pull back my legs to hit the brake and clutch simultaneously. It works. Our car stops and we avoid a serious accident. Each of the other cars just sped on as if things were normal.

After a moment of recovery, we again get going. I am driving slowly. Mom and I are talking about how difficult it is to drive here. Suddenly, I feel a searing pain in my scrotum. My first thought is that I might be having a heart attack. But then I remember, "Nah, that's not where my heart is." The intensity of the pain continues to increase. It is starting to really hurt. I don't mention anything to Mom since, again, I try not to make her worry. But the pain is becoming intense. In fact, it hurts so badly that tears are forming in my eyes and beads of sweat are breaking out on my forehead. By now I am also grimacing and shifting about in my seat. I can't figure out what the pain is, but I know that it hurts a lot!

Mom notices that something is amiss. Tears, sweating, grimaces, and rapid shifting around in one's seat provided clues that something was amiss. She asks what is wrong, and I blurt out that I'm having burning pains in my scrotum. I add that at present the pain has extended to my right leg. I even suggested that perhaps this was either some kind of weird stroke or a different kind of heart attack.

The pain was so intense that I decided to pull to the side of the road as a precaution. The car moved onto the gravel beside the road. As soon as it stopped, I reached into my pants pocket to see if I could feel anything. The inside of my pants pocket felt like shaving cream, and I instantly realized what had occurred. The Mace had been set off when I pulled back my leg to hit the brake. That knowledge led me to head back onto the highway and proceed to Hazyview as rapidly as possible. I was still hurting, but at least I knew the cause.

Once we got to Pic 'n' Pay, the main grocery store in Hazyview, I headed straight to the bathroom to assess the situation. The pain was intense but manageable. I locked myself in the bathroom, pulled down my jeans, and surveyed the damage. I won't provide specific details, but I will say that my scrotum was fiery red, as was the inner thigh of my right leg. Additionally, my right testicle was swollen to the size of a grapefruit. Overall, except for the bright red color, I looked quite "manly" on the right side.

I had to do something to alleviate the pain. So I removed a wad of paper towels, wet them in the sink, and began washing the Mace off my sensitive body parts.

An interesting tip about using Mace: always read the instructions. These instructions reveal that water interacts with the chemicals and intensifies the pain. The good news is that Pic 'n' Pay sells groceries, not guns. If they sold guns, I would have bought one instantly and either killed myself or shot off my scrotum. To paraphrase Marlow, "The pain; the pain." I was locked in the Pick 'n' Pay bathroom crying, weeping, and screaming simultaneously. Fortunately, the Pick 'n' Pay bathroom has only one toilet seat. So I was in there alone, screaming like a Maasai warrior.

Then, suddenly, after about ten minutes that seemed like an hour, the pain stopped. It subsided instantly. The Mace had worn off. My testicle was still the circumference of a grapefruit, and everything the Mace had touched was burning red, but the pain was totally gone. What to do now? Only one thing: I pulled up my pants, tightened my belt, and walked proudly into the busyness of Pic 'n' Pay. Two employees who worked close to the bathroom looked at me in wonder. But I just disappeared into the helter-skelter of the grocery business and became, like everyone else, another happy Pic 'n' Pay shopper.

Love,
Dad, Mr. Hot Pants

> PS: The swelling went down after about twelve hours. I was a little disappointed.
>
> PPS: One other challenge after this event. At Pic 'n' Pay, after you pay for your groceries, you have to walk past two armed guards who check your receipt against what you bought. Their job is to stop pilferage. I was worried that they would want to strip-search me because they thought that I had hidden a grapefruit in my pants. Fortunately, the guards either didn't notice or had no desire to search.

I share this latter story not just to entertain—although I hope it provided some comic relief within this adventure—but also to illustrate an important dimension of humility. Being humble is a state of being. It involves perspective; it means not taking yourself or your actions too seriously. Humble people can be self-deprecating without losing credibility in their own or others' eyes. The humble have the courage to admit mistakes, to laugh at themselves, and to confess that not all of their proposals and actions work out as expected. The humble even are willing to admit they are afraid.

These admissions make us more human and authentic. They also demonstrate that people can exhibit resolve and courage and still remain humble. We might fail in humiliating ways, but we have the resolve and courage to come back and try again. And resolve and courage are, as we will see soon, companions to humility. All three conditions are necessary if one wants to approach an elephant in the African bush.

CHAPTER TEN

Taking a Stand

> I learned that courage was not the absence of fear but the triumph over it. The brave man is not he who does not feel afraid, but he who conquers that fear.
> —Nelson Mandela

From a perspective of humility, it's easier to tell stories about fear than it is about courage. Fear is humbling; courage can quickly turn into arrogance.

It is inaccurate to say that Sally and I have conquered fear while living in the South African bush. We still worry about poachers, car hijackings, baboons, and lions. Additionally, we keep the sliding door closed when we feed bush babies. But it is accurate to say that we have learned to live with fear. We demonstrate that capacity by returning to Africa every year—and by feeding the bush babies every night we are there. Those actions might not demonstrate courage, but they at least show resolve and an attempt to approach a state of courage.

For eight years I had been trying to successfully approach an elephant. One elephant had followed me along the fence, but I had never successfully withstood a mock charge. My legs always took off the moment the elephant moved forward. Even the safari guides were getting tired of hearing about my repeated failures at standing firm. Some, I think, requested transfers so they didn't have to sit in the Protea television room listening to my lamentations about being unable to approach an elephant. But then, one day, things changed.

Sally was taking a nap and I was sitting on the back stoep reading. It was one of those beautiful, sunny African days that prove, according to the locals, that God loves South Africa more than most other places. He also occasionally offers us very special experiences.

> Dear Dan and Laura,
>
> I heard a small group of elephants breaking reeds in the Kruger today. I started looking and noticed that one, a female, was standing close to the fence. She was in an area where a hippo had showed up a few weeks earlier. A tree was between us, so I felt safe walking to the fence to watch her.
>
> The elephant saw me and put out her ears. As I had done so many times before, I quickly checked for dripping fluids. There were none. I looked at her rapidly and noticed that she had an identifiable feature—a large chunk was missing from the upper part of her right ear. Living in the bush is difficult, even for an elephant. The missing piece didn't bother her; she looked as if she had ample confidence in spite of the blemish. So I responded as I had been advised to do so many times before—I lowered my eyes. Next, I transitioned into a mental state that Mike Crosbie recommended: "Be humble but firm of resolve."

I don't know why, but this time the situation felt different. I wasn't just acting humble. I felt it. My first thought was that this magnificent animal has so many physical qualities that are superior to mine—size, agility, speed—along with what might be an equal number of personal characteristics superior to mine—compassion, caring, love, concern—that she really is my superior. Then another thought came to mind, a thought that changed my attitude. I suddenly realized that this experience is not a contest. We are not in competition. It isn't a matter of who has better physical or personal characteristics. It's really just a matter of being in the presence of one another. Me, an aging American business professor, and this elephant, a beautiful, magnificent creature of the African wilderness.

The other thing that happened, and I really can't explain the reason for this change, is that I didn't have a strong urge to look up. I could hear where she was. That knowledge was enough. On later reflection, I came to the realization that humble people are better listeners. At this moment I decided that if I listened, I would be safe. It wasn't necessary to see her. Humility and listening go hand in hand. And by the way, arrogance and listening are polar opposites.

Eventually, after thinking about our relationship, listening to her presence, and overall just enjoying the moment, I decided it was time to look up. The elephant was staring at me with the kindest eyes I have ever seen. She seemed to know and share my thoughts. I glanced at her briefly and then looked back down.

Another thirty seconds passed. The elephant walked around a nearby tree, looked at me again, paused, and lifted her trunk. She was smelling something, probably me, with her trunk in the air. She wasn't pulling leaves and branches from the tree. Then, in what almost seemed like a ritualistic manner, she started her charge. Her ears were flapping, and her trunk was raised. But she just didn't look frightening. In fact, even in this situation, those eyes expressed kindness.

I can't say that I stood firm because I was courageous. But neither can I say that I thought about running away. It just seemed like an action that we both understood had to take place. It was natural. The atmosphere felt similar to that which you feel when you go to lunch with a person you know has a high potential of becoming a very good friend. I just stood there, leaning on my walking stick.

At some point during this charge she crossed into a zone where it was difficult, if not impossible, for me to escape. But somehow, I didn't care. I felt certain that she wouldn't hurt me. Then, when she was about five meters away, she came to a dead stop. She continued looking straight at me, just as she had done during the mock charge. Her ears were still extended but her trunk was now lowered into a normal position. I looked up with a glance meant to show resolve but not dominance. And although it is highly dangerous to anthropomorphize a wild animal, especially an elephant, I actually thought that those kind eyes were saying: "Okay, so we've been through this together. You didn't move. That's good."

After a brief pause, the elephant gave me a final look that said, "I'll have to think about this." She then turned completely around and walked back into the bush.

I staggered back to the house, sat down on the stoep, and realized that I had just undergone one of the most exhilarating moments in my life. I was "pumped" beyond belief. It was a feeling that I have never had before. The only comparison that came to mind was what it must feel like to be a pilot who lands a jet on an aircraft carrier for the first time. It takes years of training to put yourself in a position where you have the courage to do that. But once you do it successfully, you must be exhilarated. That is how I felt sitting quietly on the back stoep.

What an experience!

I hope you folks are well.

Love,
Dad, He Who Stands with Elephants

As my pulse rate lowered and my breathing became normal, I thought about what had just happened. I concluded that my days of approaching an elephant had come to a climactic end. The goal had been achieved. Enough was enough. I had learned about the importance of humility and courage. I concluded there was nothing else to learn about approaching an elephant. I had done it. It had taken years of approaches to complete the task, but I had shown resilience and completed it. I felt good—almost smug.

Obviously, anyone who thinks in this manner still has much to learn, especially about humility. That lesson would continue very soon.

Sally and I were enjoying a quiet early afternoon sitting on the back stoep the day after this elephant encounter. I was reading while she was practicing her drawing skills. We heard the noise of an approaching elephant and soon discovered that the elephant I had approached the previous day was returning. The cuts on her ear proved who it was. She walked directly to the fence just west of the house, stopped, and stood silently under the old jackalberry tree that is on the Kruger side of the fence.

Sally asked if I was going to approach her. For some reason, it didn't feel right. The previous day's experience had been more emotionally and mentally draining than I had expected. I didn't have the energy to do it again so soon. Plus, I didn't feel the need to repeat the adventure. So I said, "No, I've had enough."

The elephant seemed nonplussed by my reluctance to return to the fence to stand with her. She showed no signs of stress or agitation. In fact, she seemed relaxed. As if to demonstrate this lack of stress, she fell sound asleep while standing beside the fence. Her eyes were closed and she was swaying side-to-side as though she were having pleasant dreams.

Suddenly, to my surprise, I began to have different desires. I wanted to go and sit beside her. It seemed natural. The incongruity was readily apparent. Earlier, when she was awake, I was unwilling to approach her. Now, while she was asleep beside the fence, I felt this strong urge to sit beside her. My emotions were conflicted.

The safari advisors had never mentioned that an elephant might come back for a second visit. Nor had they ever mentioned the possibility of an elephant falling asleep at the fence. Additionally, sitting with an elephant never was part of any of our conversations. Nor had it previously been my intention. But now it was suddenly a temptation—it was another way to "Squeeze the Juice."

It's important to admit that my strong desire to sit with her was tempered by an equal level of being afraid to do so. I did not know what might happen. What if she woke up and became startled? She might charge. Or what if she woke up, became frightened, and stepped on me? Standing close is one thing; sitting down is another. You are in a much more vulnerable position when sitting. So, after a brief debate weighing the pros and cons of going forward, I decided to play it safe. I remained on the back stoep. Sally concurred.

The elephant slept beside the fence for about ten minutes. When she awoke she looked at us briefly, reached down with her trunk and pulled some reeds from the ground, ate them, and then turned and walked slowly off into the bush. She seemed a bit disappointed.

The next morning I headed to the Protea to ask the safari guides about the experience. I specifically wondered whether I should have sat with her. The guides unanimously answered, "Yes." They said she was demonstrating trust. I needed to respond with a similar act of trust by going to sit with her.

On the one hand, I regretted not taking advantage of this rare opportunity. Not many people can say that they have sat in the wild with a sleeping African elephant. On the other hand, I complimented myself for being appropriately cautious. Fatal mistakes can occur if one trusts at the wrong time. Knowing the limitations of what you know and what you don't know about a situation is a true act of humility and a measure of safety in the African bush.

For the next few days, I remained pleased about having successfully approached an elephant but ambivalent about not having gone to sit with one while it was sleeping. The elephant didn't return. Soon we left for Johannesburg to meet our best friends from the United States, John and Mary Burke, who had come to Africa to visit us.

CHAPTER ELEVEN

Unexpected Visitors

You know you are truly alive when
you're living among lions.
—Karen Blixen, *Out of Africa*

John and Mary Burke were coming to Africa for the first time. We wanted them to have an excellent visit, so we scheduled a trip to Cape Town before we returned to Sabie Park. We were thus gone from Sabie Park for a week.

Upon returning to Sabie Park, we played the African tour guides with John and Mary. We spent three days driving in the Kruger and returned to Sabie Park at night. Next we drove deep into the Kruger and spent two nights at the Satara rest camp. We then again returned to Sabie Park and continued touring for a few days.

It had now been more than two weeks since the encounter with the elephant. We described the experience to the Burkes but suggested that the elephant's absence was proof that she had probably gone elsewhere. We even had three enjoyable but uneventful braais during this time.

Matters changed rapidly on the last night of the Burkes' visit. We planned what we hoped would be an amazing braai for their final evening in South Africa. We just didn't know how amazing it was going to be.

Dear Dan and Laura,

The Burkes leave in a couple of hours. Mom and I are going to drive them to Nelspruit to catch their flight to Johannesburg. From there they head home. It's been a most enjoyable visit, but last night was an ending no one will ever forget.

We wanted to have a special braai, so we lit the lanterns, started the fire, brought out the wine, and had a sundowner. After that we settled around the fire and planned to wait patiently for the coals to be ready to be moved. By that point, it was dark. Everything was peaceful. The day animals had made their exit, and the night animals had declared their presence and then quieted down.

But then, as we sat silently around the fire, we heard a noise that we had never before heard. It was a banging, rattling, clanging sound that was followed by the twang of a snapping wire. Just for your information, the sound of a snapping wire makes the African night particularly frightening.

Everyone looked at me when the sounds began. They thought I knew what was happening. I didn't. My initial response was confusion, but then I realized that something or someone had just broken the fence between our house and the Kruger. My first thought was poachers. In my mind, I envisioned a group of poachers trying to escape the Kruger and accidentally bumping into the fence. There was no way they would see those wires as they flashed their lights on and off coming through the bush. So they hit the fence while they were moving, hit it hard, and it snapped.

Having no other choice, I jumped up, grabbed my torch, and started shining it into the bush. If nothing else, I wanted the poachers to know that we were here and weren't running in fear. Courage, or at least the appearance of courage, seemed essential in this situation.

I couldn't see any poachers. In fact, the bush looked empty. I directed the light toward the fence and noticed the wires were pulled off their posts. Additionally, I noticed the posts were lying on the ground. Poachers could break the wires, I realized, but not even the strongest of poachers could bend those metal poles.

Then, suddenly, we heard the crackling of bush and the sound of an animal walking on the other side of the boma. Needless to say, our guests were entranced. John headed toward the house, a reasonable action, while Mary headed to the cane fence to see what she could see. Mom calmly continued tending the fire.

Mary and I directed our torches into the bush but couldn't see anything. We could hear the rattle of breaking branches and bush being destroyed, but we could not get a good glimpse of the animal. We had no doubt that it was an elephant, but we just couldn't see it through the thick bush. The rattling, thrashing, and munching sounds clearly revealed what it was.

Mary and I returned to the fire and Mom asked what I was going to do. I suggested that I should probably drive up to the gate—about a fifteen-minute drive each way—and report that an elephant had broken through the fence.

Mom's response, quite reasonable on reflection, was, "No. You're not leaving us." The way she said it indicated that this was not a debatable matter.

"But we ought to tell someone what happened," I countered.

Mom agreed and said, "Go in the house, get the portable panic button, and press it."

Now, as you know we have had an emergency panic button for the past seven years. And with some pride I say that I have never pressed it. It is nice to have "just in case," but no self-respecting bushman—even an elderly American bushman—presses a panic button unless they are about to die. So Mom and I had a lively discussion about pressing the button. I lost.

Five minutes after I pressed the button, Alfred, the head of security, comes bouncing down the driveway in a bakkie—that's African for what Americans call a pick-up truck. You could tell he was driving rapidly because his lights were careening in various directions—both side to side and up and down—as he went around the curves and over the bumps of the driveway. Soon he arrived at the house, jumped out of his bakkie, and asked, "What's wrong?" He was obviously expecting poachers, a lion in the boma, or a leopard roaming right outside.

"An elephant is stomping around right outside the boma," I replied sheepishly. Alfred looked at me with a slightly confused look, walked to the side of the boma, and shined his torch into the bush. After a few moments he saw the elephant with his light.

"Yes, it's an elephant," he said. What followed then was a rather confusing and slightly humorous exchange.

Alfred asked, "Why did you press the panic button?"

I said, "My wife made me press it. She thought you would want to know that an elephant broke through the fence."

Alfred replied, "What do you want me to do about it?"

"I don't know," I replied. "My wife insisted that I press the panic button."

I was rapidly losing my bush credibility in Alfred's eyes.

"I'm not going out there," Alfred replied. "It's dangerous."

"I agree," I replied. "I'm not going out there either."

There was a minute or so of awkward silence as Alfred and I listened to the elephant thrashing around in the bush. I broke the silence by asking him a question that cut to the core of the matter: "What should we do to stay safe?"

Alfred's answered with that standard African reply that's so important for so many situations: "Stay close to your fire." Then he added, "If you do that, you will be safe."

Staying close to your fire is such a wonderful piece of advice. Allow me, for a moment, to take off my African safari hat and put on my fatherly fedora along with my professor's miter. Lots of careers, along with the value of many companies, would be much better off had they followed this advice. I can't tell you how many times I've seen successful young businesspeople make detrimental career decisions based on the assumption that a different industry looks easier to navigate. Sometimes it is; more often, the young person discovers that this new industry or company has challenges similar to, if not more challenging than, those in the field he or she left. Only now that person has uprooted the family, perhaps lost some credibility in terms of contacts, and probably stymied or at least slowed down his or her career progression.

But it is not just young business people who stray too far from their fire. Research shows that 82 percent of acquisitions that companies make outside of their fields of expertise are non-accretive. In other words, companies often lose money when they buy companies outside their areas of knowledge. Put simply, the acquiring companies should stay close to their fire and make acquisitions in areas they understand. Business leaders could learn useful information by spending more time in the African bush.

But I digress. Back to the bush. Follow Alfred's advice we did. All of us stayed within one meter of the fire for the remainder of the braai. Then, when the food was fully cooked, we dashed cheetah-like into the house.

The elephant continued to tromp around for the remainder of the evening. This morning I noticed the fence is destroyed, but there is no sign of the elephant, except for an enormous pile of poop parked in the driveway. It was so large that Mary and I had to use a shovel to remove it—otherwise, the top of the pile would have hit the bottom of the car.

That's all for now. The Burkes leave in ten minutes.

I hope you folks are well.

Love,
Dad, the Panic-Button Pusher

We were never able to determine if the elephant that broke through the fence was the same one I had previously approached. Sally and I both believe that it was. But that is an emotional response. We have no proof. No additional visits from the elephant took place for the remainder of this visit.

Mike and Lynda Crosbie spent a week at the bush house that October and reported that an elephant broke through the fence while they were staying at the house. Mike took a picture of her as she was peeking over the cane fence. The picture missed the notch in her right ear but clearly showed her loving, gentle eyes. So we are certain that she did eventually return. Our only thought, as we looked at the picture Mike sent, was that we hoped the elephant was having a wonderful year.

The broken fence did, however, provide an additional adventure before we departed for the season. It was 6:45 a.m. on the Tuesday after the Burkes had left. We were planning to fly back to the United States on Wednesday. So the schedule for the day involved packing, preparing the house to be closed for ten months, and a final invigorating walk around the confines of Sabie Park. I take such a walk just about every day.

The sun, which had just cleared the horizon, provided a smidgen of early morning light, when my fear of unknown noises returned: someone was knocking at the carport door. The noise startled me, but then I remembered, as I walked toward the door, that poachers would probably not knock. This realization somewhat mitigated the fear. Still, my heart was pounding as I pulled back the curtains to see who was knocking. Earnest, the game manager, was standing on the steps. He was alone. I calmly opened the door.

Earnest said that he came to make sure that I did not take my daily morning walk. I said, "Okay," but then asked, "Why not?" A final trip with my "walking stick" was on the agenda for our last full day in Sabie Park.

Earnest's reply removed all debate. "A pride of lions came across the broken fence last night," Earnest replied. "They killed a young zebra just beyond your driveway and are now eating it. I suspect they will stay in the area for a while once they finish breakfast."

Even the slightest desire for a year-end walk evaporated with Ernest's news. I did, however, want to witness the event. So I woke Sally and we drove to the scene. By the time we arrived, the lions had eaten their fill and were lounging in the area near the dead zebra. Six lions were lying near the body. Two others were lying off in the bush. Three of the lions were asleep; the others were awake but seemed to have little desire to move. Two hyenas crouched nearby, waiting for their turn at the carcass.

The threat to the other animals in Sabie Park was minimal since lions go over a week between meals. This pride was obviously stuffed. We checked on the lions throughout the day. They continued to look immobile. Lions sleep between fifteen and twenty hours a day, with the reported average being about eighteen. This pride was helping to maintain that average.

We did two more checks on the lions before leaving the next morning. The pride had moved toward the fence that separates Sabie Park from the public highway. This location trapped the pride so the lions were now a bigger threat than before. While one always maintains a healthy respect for Kruger's predators, the animals tend not to be as dangerous as those found in zoos and other enclosures. This reduced danger in the wild sounds counterintuitive, but the explanation is simple: when wild animals have a means of escape, they choose that option. Thus, in the vast majority of encounters, predators will walk away rather than engage with humans. When cornered, however, predators become vicious. It's a good idea to stay far away from cornered animals.

I talked briefly with Earnest before we left for Johannesburg. He and his staff were closely monitoring the lions' movements and had made the decision to get assistance from Kruger's Wildlife Services. Kruger representatives were expected to arrive within a few hours. The lions would then be darted and moved back into the Kruger at a safe distance from Sabie Park.

Sally and I took a brief side trip along the public road that borders the fence as we left for the year. The pride was still trapped there. The Kruger officials would have to be careful. A few days after returning home, we learned through email that the lions had been darted and safely removed from the area.

CHAPTER TWELVE

Sitting with Elephants and Chasing Leopards

Only those who risk going too far can
possibly find out how far one can go.
—T. S. Eliot

The end-of-the-year lion encounter provided a dramatic conclusion to our previous visit. Yet the focus of our off-season conversations continued to be on the elephant that I had successfully approached. We even began to refer to her as "Our Elephant."

Initially, we wondered whether we would ever see Our Elephant again. As the discussions proceeded, however, we came to the conclusion that the encounter with "our" elephant had probably run its course. I had successfully approached her but had missed the opportunity to sit beside her when she was sleeping. It was one of those opportunities in life that, once missed, never comes again.

Elephants travel up to fifty kilometers a day and migrate thousands of kilometers in a year. The range that elephants' travel is so vast that two or more years often pass before they return to a previously visited location. We thus returned the following year with the hope that we would get to see elephants in our backyard, but we had little expectation that we would see Our Elephant again. Our main hope was that we might someday see her while we were traveling in the Kruger.

To our delight, a herd of twenty elephants briefly visited the back fence within a week of our arrival. We searched to identify Our Elephant but were unable to do so. The next day, however, a smaller herd of elephants came to the fence.

Dear Dan and Laura,

The African sojourners are online.

Highlights so far. The first, and by far the most impressive, was the return of the elephant. Yesterday, Friday, we were cleaning the house and getting ready for the Stricklands to visit. I looked outside while sweeping and saw an elephant standing right beside the fence. She was munching on tree branches and staring at the house. I looked carefully and realized that it was Our Elephant. The tusk alignment, the body markings, and the distinct cut on her ear confirmed her identity. I was excited to see her again.

I got Mom, and we both went out and sat on the back stoep. We did not, of course, stare at her. We looked down and only occasionally glanced up.

Our Elephant kept looking at us and seemed to be waiting

for something. I thought that perhaps she wanted me to approach, but I was not at all certain that was her message. One must renew old friendships with caution, especially when that friendship is with a wild African elephant.

Then, lo and behold, a baby elephant trots out of the bush about two meters behind "our" elephant. The baby couldn't have been more than a few weeks old. Following the baby was another young elephant, probably a few years old, and a larger, full-grown elephant. Mom quickly caught the gist of what was going on with the observation, "She's showing us her family." And by gosh, I think Mom was right. After the family passed, "our" elephant looked at us, backed up a few steps, and then headed with her brood toward the river. A shiver went down my spine after I realized what had happened.

A second highlight happened earlier today. The Stricklands left today at about 11:00. Lonnie and Kitty are always gracious visitors, and they gave us some young impala lilies as departing gifts. We placed the lilies on the back stoep.

Later in the afternoon we decided to take a ride in the Kruger along the Sabie River. We planned to exit at the Pilablani gate around 5:30 p.m. and then drive fifteen kilometers to Hazyview to have dinner. We saw no animals on the drive, but the scenery along the river made for a very enjoyable drive.

As we were leaving the bush house, a troop of baboons darted across the driveway. I shouted "You bastards, the house is locked!!" Then I returned and double and triple checked the doors to make sure that what I had said was true.

You have probably already guessed what happened. When we returned from Hazyview, we found dirt strewn all across the back stoep. The baboons had pulled the impala lilies from their containers and had eaten the roots of each plant.

I decided to clean the mess before going to sleep. As I was sweeping dirt from the back stoep, I heard water running. The sound came from the side of the house, not the back area where the Sabie River flows. A little investigation led to the discovery that the baboons, those bastards, had turned on the water in the outside sink. It was running full blast.

There is, however, one note of joy within this scenario. The baboons only turned on the hot water. So perhaps they burnt their blood-sucking mouths to a crisp!!!

By the way, as you may remember, the elephants knocked down the fence around the lapa and the outside shower while we were gone last year. Bennie, the head of maintenance, rebuilt it. He did a fantastic job. It looks wonderful. We now even have a lapa door that latches.

I hope you folks are well.

Love,

Dad, the Nursery Curator

PS: Five extra dollars in the will to the first of you who can explain the complex pun of the above signature.

A visit from the elephant herd this early in the season rekindled our enthusiasm for future visits. We wondered if the elephant we had labeled "ours" would return again. Additionally, if she did return, we wondered if I would get a second chance to sit with her. The presence of those babies complicated matters. I wasn't sure that she wanted me close when they were nearby. We also wondered if Our Elephant would return alone, with the herd, or with this small splinter group. In only a few days we had answers to these questions.

Dear Laura and Dan,

This morning we went to the Protea for breakfast and then headed back to the bush house. Our plans were to rest a bit and then drive into Hazyview for supplies. When we got back from the Protea, Mom noticed some elephants far off in the Kruger. We watched for a few minutes and noticed that they were moving toward our house. So we waited.

Soon, in what seemed like no time at all, we had a herd of twelve elephants, two of which were babies, standing in the open space beside our fence. Three of the adult elephants had fallen asleep, as had the two babies. The herd obviously felt safe.

Our Elephant was not in the group. It is highly probable, however, that this was part of her herd. I base that observation on the knowledge that herds tend to disperse and then come back together. These elephants seemed too comfortable with the setting not to have been here before. Additionally, the two babies looked very much like the ones we had seen earlier in the presence of "our" elephant.

I felt a strong calling to take the next step, so I rose from my chair and began walking slowly toward the herd. I kept my eyes cast downward as I traveled. I did, of course, surreptitiously glance up to make sure I wasn't disturbing the herd. None of the elephants moved, nor did any seem bothered. My goal was to get to a tree that was about five meters from the herd.

I sat down once I got to the tree. Each of the adult elephants looked at me, even the three that were sleeping. It seems that elephants don't sleep soundly—they wake up, glance around, and then close their eyes and go back to sleep.

I kept looking at the ground and only occasionally glanced at the herd. No one seemed disturbed by my presence. The situation seemed safe, especially since the babies were situated toward the back of the herd. It did, though, seem important to remain in a sitting position. To stand would have upset the balance of the arrangement.

After about fifteen minutes, I decided it was time to get closer. So I started scooting forward on my butt. That is why I am still pulling thistles from my pants. I moved slowly but deliberately with my eyes on the ground. Four of the elephants watched, but none gave any signal of being bothered. In the end, I managed to "butt scoot" all to the way to the fence. At this point it seemed smart to stop. The presence of the fence seemed to give solace to the elephants—and to me as well. I had no desire to go under it—nor would it have been wise to do so.

The bottom line—no pun intended on my thorn-filled butt—is that I managed to sit approximately one meter away from a magnificent herd of wild African elephants. The entire herd seemed unperturbed by my presence. It was mesmerizing. I sat with them for about an hour.

I have to note, though, that the feeling of sitting with the herd was quite different from that which occurred last year when I approached an elephant and withstood a mock charge. Whereas last year's feeling was similar to landing a fighter jet on an aircraft carrier—the adrenaline was over the top—this year's feeling was one of extreme calm. The adrenaline glands were in neutral. Sitting there felt natural, almost homey. Although I was cautious, I never felt afraid or threatened. The elephants seemed comfortable with me as well.

Eventually, the adult elephants awoke, as did one of the babies. The other baby was still asleep. Gradually, in no particular rush, the adult elephants began wandering away from the fence and moving slowly back into the Kruger. Two adult elephants stayed close to the sleeping baby. After she awoke, one of the two pushed the baby with her trunk, and the threesome walked off sprightly in the direction of the herd.

My feeling after the event concluded was one of thankfulness. I felt as if I had gotten a second chance after missing last year's opportunity. It is not often that life hands you a second chance. When it does, it's a good idea to grab it. Even better, I realized that this second chance may have been better than the first one that I missed. I got to sit with an entire herd, not just a single elephant. Perhaps it pays to wait.

I hope you folks are well.

Love,
Dad, He Who Sits with Elephants

Herds or portions of the herd returned nine more times that winter. I sat with them on each occasion. Our Elephant participated in seven of the nine appearances. As we observed the herd more and more, we came to the conclusion that Our Elephant was the herd's matriarch. Where she went, others followed. What she wanted to do, others did as well. Overall, she was dictating the herd's behavior. Her role may have made it easier for me to sit with the herd. She was obviously granting me permission.

The matriarch is the leader of the elephant family. The oldest female in the family usually holds the position. The matriarch determines when and where the herd travels to find food. The identification of these food sites depends on the matriarch's memory of previous visits to the areas. Hence, even though it may have been two years or longer since the matriarch had visited a site, her job is to remember where food was previously available.

The matriarch additionally dictates whether the herd stays together as a single unit or divides temporarily into sub-units while it searches for food and water. She even determines when the herd will leave a watering site. If you ever observe a herd of elephants at a watering location, you can easily identify the matriarch. She is the one who walks away first. Gradually, but in complete compliance, other elephants follow in her direction. Overall, the matriarch accepts responsibility for taking care of the herd, including making sure that mothers of young calves get ample water to stimulate their milk production.

Our Elephant's position within the herd proved especially helpful during the herd's fifth visit. I was sitting comfortably about three meters from the herd when I noticed an adolescent male moving toward me from the back of the herd. The air of aggressiveness was unmistakable. His ears were pinned against his head and he moved in my direction in a determined manner. Basically, he would take two or three aggressive steps forward and then pause and stare at me. I tried to give the impression of looking at the ground rather than staring back at him. I did not want to challenge him. I did, however, glance frequently in his direction and monitor his movements toward me. No fluid was coming from the glands beneath his ears.

This was the first time in my elephant-sitting experience that I felt endangered. It seemed as if this adolescent was going to try to prove himself. I was not sure how this proving would take place, but none of the options I pondered seemed good. I contemplated butt-scooting backward, and I mentally reviewed a plan to jump up abruptly, wave my arms, and try to scare the elephant away.

In the midst of examining these alternatives, I noticed Our Elephant moving toward me as well. Initially, she had been about fifteen meters away, eating tree leaves. Now she was coming toward me with a determined purpose. Her ears were wide apart. She turned when she got within ten meters of me and walked directly toward the adolescent elephant. He was about the same distance away. As she turned, Our Elephant lowered her head while simultaneously pulling her ears back against her body. She then sped up and bumped firmly into the adolescent elephant. The adolescent stumbled sideways, paused, and then received a second blow from Our Elephant. It was readily apparent that Our Elephant was pushing the adolescent in the opposite direction. She was saying, "Leave him alone; don't go testing your manhood against him." Perhaps she was even saying, "He's one of ours." Whatever the message, the adolescent understood. He walked obediently to the rear of the herd.

Our Elephant glanced at me and then walked back to the position where she had previously been. She resumed pulling on branches and munching leaves. I noticed during my furtive glances that she continued to keep an eye on me. The tone felt protective. Mentally, I said, "Thanks. I owe you one." She seemed to understand the message.

As the visits continued I noticed that I was tending more and more to interpret the elephant's behavior from a human perspective. These tendencies are probably inevitable when you are interacting frequently with animals; however, they can also be dangerous. A single misinterpretation can have fatal consequences. The rational side of my brain was in a constant war with the pattern-recognition side. The former contended that the matriarch's push of the adolescent elephant was coincidental; the latter interpreted these behaviors as protective. Both sides made a good case.

Mike and Lynda Crosbie visited a few days after the incident with the adolescent elephant. Our herd came to visit one afternoon while Mike was dozing on our back stoep. I had previously been ambivalent about sitting with the herd in front of Mike. I had described the experience to Mike, but I was concerned that I might be trying to arrogantly display my connection with the elephants if I actually sat with them while Mike was watching. I did not want to define the elephant relationship in that way. Showmanship is in stark contrast to humility. Additionally, I considered these elephant encounters a private affair.

Since Mike was sleeping, however, I thought it might be possible to slip down to the fence and sit briefly with the herd before he awoke. I did so for about twenty minutes. One young elephant seemed particularly interested in me and came pretty close. At one point, we were probably two meters apart. I just kept sitting, looking down, and feeling humble. The elephant posed no threat and eventually moved back into the bush.

When I got back to the stoep, I discovered that Mike had awoken and had viewed most of the event. He seemed to enjoy watching the experience as much as I enjoyed participating in it.

Mike observed that the herd was obviously comfortable with me. He said that he had been worried about my safety upon hearing what I had been doing. Now that he had watched an encounter, however, he expressed the belief that I had little risk. He encouraged me to keep sitting with the herd, adding, again, that the elephants had obviously gotten to know me. He further added that he thought they would remember me.

Mike then gave me a piece of advice that I had been contemplating vaguely but had not really formalized in my mind. Stated simply, Mike suggested that I should control my thoughts while sitting with the herd. Specifically, he advised me to think only positive thoughts when I was with them. He added further that I should consider the elephants as being able to understand my thoughts.

Mike's advice was easy to accept since my mind was already moving in that direction. It was a small step from thinking thoughts that the elephants might understand to conversing with the elephants in my thoughts. Obviously, my belief system was moving beyond anthropomorphizing (i.e., attributing human personality to the elephants) to trying to communicate with them mentally. From a bigger perspective, I found myself rapidly moving toward believing that I was at one with the elephants and with the entire African bush.

But the rational side didn't give up easily—nor should it have. A subsequent event provided a reminder that being "at one" with the bush can be hazardous.

The following event occurred the day after Mike and Lynda left.

> Dear Dan and Laura:
>
> Mom and I were sitting and relaxing on the stoep this afternoon. We heard a couple of impalas barking furiously and then saw a huge kudu run rapidly away from the spot of the barking. We kept looking into the bush, and then, suddenly, a beautiful leopard emerged. He was walking in the Kruger about three meters from the fence.
>
> The leopard was obviously on the hunt and paid no attention to us. He disappeared into the reeds about twenty

seconds after we saw him. He was heading toward Sabie Park's picnic area.

I remained with Mom on the back stoep for a few minutes, but then I couldn't stand it any longer. I had to follow him. So I started walking along the fence to see if I could locate where the leopard had gone. Mom objected to my doing this, but I promised to be extremely careful. Plus, I had my walking stick.

I traversed along the fence for about five hundred meters but couldn't see any sign of the leopard. The vision in this part of the bush is severely limited because of the heavy reeds. In fact, the reeds go all the way to the Sabie River.

Then, suddenly, as I was standing at the crest of a small hill that overlooks the scene, I noticed that the reeds, which were about thirty meters from the fence, were beginning to shake. Immediately thereafter, an African fish eagle squawked loudly and flew into the air. Soon, two bushbucks barked and ran full speed through the reeds toward the Sabie River.

The leopard had just tried to make a kill. The silence that followed indicated that she had failed. Noises of a struggle or of a dying animal would be noticeable if the leopard had caught its prey. Instead, the bush was quiet, eerily so. Then, almost imperceptibly, I noticed the reeds begin to move. The leopard had changed direction. She was walking away from the Sabie River toward where I was. We were still twenty meters apart, but the leopard was obviously moving in my direction. Leopards, by the way, are stealth hunters. Unlike cheetahs, they sneak up on their prey.

It was at this moment that I remembered that this is not Disney World. This leopard really was hunting. She was not hunting me—she had not yet seen me. If she had, she would have been moving faster. But she was obviously seeking prey in my direction. Additionally, I was certain that if she were hungry enough, she would change menu options based on what was available. I preferred not to be on that menu.

So, without further ado, I skedaddled back to the bush house. I traveled silently but as quickly as I could. Remember, a key rule of the bush is "Never Run." So I didn't. However, I added an important clause to that rule: "Never Run; but Don't Dawdle, Either."

After I arrived safely at the bush house, I decided the Never-Run-but-Don't-Dawdle-Either canard needs a third observation. So here is the entire saying: "Never Run but Don't Dawdle Either; and Never Follow a Hungry Leopard." It sounds like good advice to me.

I hope you folks are well.

Love,
Dad, the Leopard-Chasing Elephant-Sitter

After the leopard experience had concluded, I sat on a recliner on the back stoep and pondered how my bush behavior had changed over the years. A decade earlier we had excitedly but safely watched a leopard in the driveway from the safety of our car. The windows were closed and the doors were locked. Now I had chosen to follow the leopard on foot with only a walking stick for protection.

Further reflections on these events, however, especially those that focused on the ending moments of this recent leopard encounter, led to the realization that tracking that leopard was a huge mistake. I was fortunate to not get hurt. My feeling at one with the elephants, along with a growing belief that I could communicate with them, caused me to slide from humility into hubris: I began to egocentrically believe that I was one with the bush and everything in it. This assumption led to the dangerously arrogant belief that I understood what animals were thinking. I was even starting to assume that I had the ability to communicate with them. These assumptions were not just arrogant; they were foolhardy. They led to foolish behavior on my part. I therefore vowed to become more circumspect from that moment forward. I would continue to direct positive thoughts toward the elephants, but I would do so from the humble perspective that my thoughts might not be conveyed as clearly and as accurately as I meant them to be. Additionally, I made a commitment to never again go into the bush attempting to direct my thoughts toward predators.

As previously noted, the elephant-sittings continued throughout the summer. The elephants continued to display evidence that we were forming a bond. On two occasions the herd, led by Our

Elephant, paraded babies along the fence in front of me. Interestingly, on both of these occasions, the herd walked along the fence in one direction and then turned and walked back in the opposite direction. It was easy to interpret their intentions: they were showing me the family. On each occasion, remembering Mike Crosby's advice, I expressed mental admiration for the family. The specific thoughts that I repeated were: "You have such a beautiful family," and "Your children are gorgeous." We had discovered that it is not just humans who are proud of their young; elephants are too.

Two particular events occurred during this period, both of which still seem unbelievable. The first event occurred a week before we left. I was sitting with the full herd, but half the elephants were sleeping by the time I worked my way into the sitting position. But this time something different happened: three of the elephants that were awake started moving slowly toward the fence. They seemed in no rush; in fact, they seemed almost lackadaisical. Then, when they got three meters from the fence, they cautiously lowered their front legs, then their back legs. Then, with no further ado, each lay down right beside the fence. They didn't just plop down. Instead, they just gradually tipped onto their sides. Each of the three kept at least one eye open.

I looked on in amazement. Much like the previous year, when I instinctively knew to go and sit with that sleeping elephant but didn't, I again knew instinctively what to do. But this time I did not hesitate. So, without further consideration, I lay down beside the elephants. Right in the grass. I felt no danger from the elephants. My only concern was with bugs and other insects that inhabited the nearby grasses. I was aware of the consequences of the bug bites, but I decided that the experience was worth the risk. So I reclined in the grass.

There we were: ten tons of elephant and two hundred pounds of human lying side by side in the bush, two meters apart. "Our" elephant watched this event while standing five meters away. She seemed to approve. We "slept" together for fifteen minutes. Full disclosure, I didn't sleep.

Eventually, the elephants got up, walked back to the herd, and the matriarch, Our Elephant, led them off toward the Sabie River. I returned to the back stoep and soon discovered my legs were covered with bug bites. Fortunately, other than discomfort from itching, I suffered no long-term health consequences from the bites. The experience was well worth it.

The second "unbelievable" event occurred on the final day of our visit.

Dear Dan and Laura,

Greetings from the Air France Sky Club in Johannesburg. This year's visit is a wrap. I just want to document an event from the final day.

The entire herd showed up this morning as we were preparing to close the house. You've read the story throughout the summer, so I won't go into detail again. Suffice it to say that I sat and lay with the herd for the better part of an hour. This time, however, I was the one who ended the event. I left before they did. We had to finish shutting down the house.

So I returned to the house and began taking down the lanterns and moving chairs from the lapa into the house. The elephants continued to "mill around" during these activities.

My last outside act was to move the chaise lounges and plastic tables from the back stoep into the house. As I did so, I glanced at the herd and noticed the movements were becoming more intentional. In fact, the elephants seemed to be lining up.

Being intrigued by this activity, I got Mom and we returned to the back stoep and watched. By now the entire herd was in a straight line along the fence. The matriarch was at the front of the line. She then proceeded to walk beside the fence for two meters, then turned to her right and walked straight into the bush. The other elephants followed her path.

We have never seen them leave in such a purposeful, organized manner. Perhaps they were saying "goodbye." Or perhaps they were acknowledging that this winter's visit was over and they knew we would be leaving. I suspect that they might have been indicating that they would be leaving too. Darn, this is fascinating but confusing.

All in all, a strange last day. It's probably important that we get back to the United States and get our heads adjusted. We may have gotten too involved with the elephants.

Additionally, it is possible that the elephants have gotten too involved with us. We both might need "time out."

It's going to be difficult to explain these events to people at home. I'm not sure that I'm going to do so. Rational people might say, "You've lost it." Perhaps we have.

I hope you folks are well.

Love,
Dad Who Needs a Counselor

This summer of sitting with the elephants was a special one. Unlike the previous year, when the lions diverted our attention just before we left, the focus for the following year's visit remained on the elephants.

The biggest challenge during the "sitting" visits was more mental than physical. I had allowed myself to go beyond reason in terms of how I was interpreting the elephants' behavior. The "sitting visits" had a dream-like feel both as they occurred and afterward as I reflected on them. They resembled conditions similar to those described by people who take strong medications for a serious illness. Often, these people report having a difficult time separating experiences that actually happened from those about which they have dreamt. Each day in the bush felt that way. In the morning, I would ask myself if I had really sat with a herd of elephants yesterday or if it was just a dream. Then the day would go on, an elephant opportunity would resurface, and I was back in the swing of sitting with elephants.

For better or worse, the confusion lessened toward the end of the visit. The bug bites on my legs verified that I had been lying with elephants. The constant need to scratch assured me that what I thought happened, had happened.

The interactions with the elephant herd throughout the summer led to a fuller understanding of what it takes to sit with a herd of elephants. Interestingly, the techniques for sitting differ slightly from those used to approach an elephant.

Humility, again, is the essential ingredient. Each elephant recognizes and responds favorably to it. As before, the approach toward the herd is done without staring. Remember, only predators stare.

Humble thoughts cause the head to be pointed downward, with the gaze directed toward the ground. Humble thoughts accompany all movements.

You gradually lower your body as you move toward the herd. The movement is similar to that of a supplicant moving toward a source of extreme power. The closer you get to the herd, the lower your body becomes. By the time you are within five meters of the herd, the majority of your body should be close to the ground. This lowered position makes the transition from walking to sitting seamless.

You move into the sitting position slowly and without concerns of being vulnerable. You have courage. Simultaneously, as you sit, you are demonstrating high levels of humility and trust since the elephants have the full advantage. Over time I found it best to think of these actions as lowering myself in the elephant's presence, a humble act. And, again, you must always remember that you trust the elephant not to take advantage of the situation. Your level of vulnerability is inexpressibly high once you sit.

I have never approached a herd by walking upright. That stance is too aggressive. Instead, as already mentioned, a sitting position within five meters of the herd works effectively. After that, all forward movement occurs through butt-scooting. The elephants understand the symbolism of the position. With regard to lying down, the elephants initiate that action. Only do so after the elephants first lie down.

The issue of a mock charge never surfaced during a sitting encounter. The elephants move toward and away during the visits, but their movements are slow and deliberate. None imply a threat, with the exception of the encounter with the adolescent elephant. Perhaps the mock charges stopped because the elephants recognized and had become familiar with me. Or perhaps the act of lowering myself before getting too close removed the threat that triggered a charge. No matter. All that I can state is that the mock charges disappeared.

It is also important to note that a "language of permission" evolved as I learned to move closer to the herd. Stated simply, each time as I "butt-scooted" closer to the herd, I paused to make sure the elephants were not upset by my efforts to move closer. The pause following the movement was a way to seek permission for the just-completed move. This pause for permission was meant respectfully. During the pause, I waited for any indication that I had come too close. Although I never received an indication that I had done so, I had a planned retreat if any elephant sent such a signal.

Finally, it is important to highlight the ongoing presence of the fence. It was always there. I never crossed the fence to move toward the herd, nor did the elephants show any desire to cross the fence and move toward me. In my mind, the fence provided a barrier of protection for both of us. Good fences make good neighbors.

We left Sabie Park that summer highly anticipating our return the following year. We were, by now, fully convinced that the elephants would be waiting for us. I was so enthralled by our experiences that I put together a presentation entitled "How to Sit with a Herd of Elephants." My initial plan was to deliver it at local events such as luncheons, after-dinner speeches, and so forth. However, the presentation was so well received that I began delivering it throughout the United States as well as in Finland, Sweden, Singapore, and Zanzibar. Lots of people are interested in sitting with elephants. The presentation even got turned into a TEDx Talk that thousands of people have viewed.

The presentation highlights the experiences described so far. It is supported with pictures that Sally took the last time the elephants visited. On the topic of pictures, I should add that I took no photographs during any of my visits with the elephants. It seemed inappropriate. The visits were personal encounters. I already had the email descriptions sent to our children to remember the events. Pictures seemed redundant.

A few Sabie Park residents learned that I was sitting with elephants and asked to watch and take pictures. I said no. This relationship was private, not public. I knew I was becoming a crotchety old man, but I didn't care. Fortunately, on the day of the last visit from the elephants, Sally brought out a camera and took pictures unbeknownst to me. It has proven useful that she did. The pictures become a point of interest in the presentations.

In one of the earliest presentations of "How to Sit with a Herd of Elephants," an event delivered to graduate students at the University of Alabama, one of the attendees, Michael Oczypok, asked an unexpected question. He inquired, "Where do you go from here?" The question took me aback. The answer to that question had never occurred to me. It seemed as if I would continue sitting with the elephants for as long as we returned to South Africa. There was no future goal—I just naïvely believed we would go on like this forever.

After pondering Michael's question for a moment, I answered with what seemed like two realistic goals: First, I would like to crawl under the fence and join the elephants with no barriers between us. Second, I would like the matriarch to touch me with her trunk. This second experience, the act of having a wild elephant touch you with its trunk, is described in *The Elephant Whisperer*.

I was pleased with this off-the-cuff answer. Others in attendance were impressed with the response and commented on my bravery. There was lots of applause, handshaking, thanks for doing the presentation, and other acknowledgments of gratitude. Many said that they wished that they could do what my wife and I were doing.

But one must always be careful. Accolades contain a hidden danger. Unless one is appropriately cautious, each accolade can sneakily chip away at one's humility.

CHAPTER THIRTEEN

A Little Monkey Business

"Hello, companion," said Magnus.
The monkey made a terrible sound, half snarl and half hiss.
"I begin to rather doubt the beauty of
our friendship," said Magnus.
—Cassandra Clare, *The Bane Chronicles*

Chapter 13

We returned to Sabie Park in June of the following year. We were eager to get back to the bush and especially to see if the elephants were waiting for us in the backyard. We were sure Our Elephant would visit as soon as we arrived.

To our chagrin, only two small herds came to the fence in the first five weeks. One of these herds had seven elephants; the other had five. Neither contained Our Elephant.

I sat with both herds and found the experience invigorating. However, the connection with the herds felt different. No bond developed with these groups. The elephants responded as if I were an impala, kudu, warthog, or any other nonthreatening animal meandering nearby. They glanced at me, decided I was not a threat, and then ignored me and went about their business. We came to the conclusion that last year's herd, along with Our Elephant, had departed to other parts of the Kruger.

Elephants, like many animals, break into smaller groups and separate when the herd becomes too large. Nature and the environment demand this course of action. An elephant eats between three hundred and five hundred pounds of vegetation a day. An entire herd, therefore, strains the local environment. As the herd grows, food sources become stressed. Dispersion becomes a necessity.

Our backyard area provided visible evidence of what elephants can do to an area. When we arrived for this year's visit, we noticed that reeds, which had been abundant the previous summer, were now gone from the area immediately behind the fence. There were still some reeds off in the distance, but the ground beside the fence was barren. Additionally, the lower parts of trees were stripped of bark, and numerous branches had been broken off and lay on the ground without leaves. There were still enough leaves high in the tree to provide protective shade for the herd, but the food source was gone. The elephants had decimated the area.

Our daughter, Laura, and our eight-year-old granddaughter, Ella, visited for a week soon after our arrival. Unfortunately, no elephants came to the fence during their visit. This absence was particularly problematic since we had all but guaranteed a visit from Our Elephant when persuading them to visit. Part of my persuasion to get Laura to visit involved the rationale that Our Elephant had shown us her family; it therefore seemed appropriate to show her ours. We even discussed the possibility of Laura and Ella sitting with the herd. No commitments were made on this matter, but hopes were high.

Needless to say, deep disappointment surfaced when no elephants came to the fence. We had obviously oversold the possibility of getting to sit with a herd of elephants.

To alleviate the disappointment, we permitted Ella to give a banana to a monkey who stopped by each morning. Ella would place the banana in the nearby jackalberry tree and the monkey would scoot down, grab it, and then dash up the tree to enjoy its reward.

The monkey continued to appear each morning after Ella returned to the United States. I felt guilty about the habit we had developed, so I continued to give the monkey a daily banana. Overall, it was not a good idea.

Dear Ella,

I just had an encounter with your monkey that I have to share with you. Here's what happened.

Early this morning I poured a bowl of breakfast cereal and put it on the table on the back stoep. I then went into the house to get milk for the cereal. As you know, I was following my morning ritual.

As I was returning to the stoep with the milk, I saw your monkey reach onto the table, grab the bowl of cereal, and walk away holding it in his two front paws. I really like the cereal bowl she grabbed, so I shouted and started running after the monkey. She sped up and ran to the side of the house carrying the bowl with the cereal.

Now, I have to admit that what happened next had to look pretty silly. I chased after the monkey, and she kept running along the side of the house, carrying the bowl. As you know, I still have pretty good speed, so I was catching up with her. However, full confession, monkeys don't go too fast when running upright on two legs while also carrying a bowl of cereal.

So here's the picture: in the remote African bush, we see a monkey running with a bowl of cereal in her hands and a sixty-seven-year-old man chasing after her shouting, "Put down that bowl!" It had to look silly to anyone who might have seen it.

I caught up with her by the time she got to the carport. But when I did, I realized I had another problem: how to get the bowl back. I was certain she would bite me if I simply reached for it.

I was looming over the monkey while trying to resolve this problem, but she didn't recognize my conundrum. Instead, she panicked at my presence, threw the bowl in the air, and ran to the far side of the carport. The bowl broke, and there is now cereal and glass all over the carport.

The monkey and I had one last confrontation. I yelled at her and said, "I've given you bananas every day for over a month! This is how you pay me back? You'll never get another banana from me!!"

Her response? She made a nasty growl, showed her teeth, and said, I guess, "I prefer cereal."

I hope you are well.

Love,
Bada, the Monkey Racer

PS: A herd of cape buffalo are eating right beside the fence as I type this note. I wonder if cape buffalo like bananas.

***

Dear Ella,

A quick monkey update. After yesterday's monkey confrontation, I thought your monkey would be gone forever. Wrong! Read on!

This morning I was fixing breakfast for myself. I planned on using the grill on the back stoep to make some bacon and eggs. I took plates and eggs outside and went back into the house to get the bacon.

Without thinking, I left the sliding door open as I walked into the house. I got the bacon from the refrigerator, turned, and found YOUR MONKEY standing in the house, leaning against the couch. She had one paw against the couch while the other was on her hip. Her legs were crossed. She looked as if she was asking, "Well, what are we fixing for breakfast today?"

Seeing your monkey in the house startled me. I jumped

in surprise. Then, when I realized where she was, I shouted, "Get out of here! Get out of this house!" She didn't move, so I grabbed a butcher knife from the kitchen counter and took after her. That made her move.

So the picture of today's event has to look just about as funny as yesterday's. Today we have a sixty-seven-year-old man waving a butcher knife above his head while chasing a monkey out the door. There seem to be a lot of chase scenes in these stories.

The monkey ran outside, climbed high in the jackalberry tree, and started chattering at me.

After it was all over, I woke up Nana to tell her what happened. She listened and had a typical Nana reaction: "Give her a banana." I ended up giving her three.

That monkey is going to be the death of me yet.

Love,
Bada, the Monkey Magnet

***

Dear Ella,

Your monkey . . . grrrrr. I was cleaning the food pantry cabinets earlier today. I moved the food onto the kitchen table. On the table were bananas, oranges, a jar of peanut butter, and an unopened loaf of bread.

I heard a noise as I was going back to the cabinet to wipe it clean. I turned and saw your monkey running away with the loaf of bread. I chased her out of the door, but I couldn't catch her. She climbed high in the jackalberry tree and is now sitting there eating the entire loaf of bread.

It surprised me that she took the bread rather than the bananas. I guess she likes to alter her diet. Sadly, that was the last loaf of bread we have in the house. I was planning to have a peanut butter sandwich for lunch. Oh well, I guess I'll just eat bananas.

Your monkey . . . grrrrrrr!!

Love,
Bada, the Breadless

For clarification purposes, I should add that Ella, as the oldest grandchild in our family, got the honor of designating names for her grandparents. When she was six months old, she pointed at me and said, "Bada." I instantly adopted the name and have worn it with pride ever since. When Ella and the other grandchildren get older, I will ask them to begin calling me by my African name. But that's a story for later.

Our South African friends Mike and Lynda Crosbie came for a visit in the middle of July. Our Elephant and her herd had still failed to materialize. We saw elephants in the distance and we saw them on drives into the Kruger, but the area beside the fence remained bereft of elephants.

All of us agreed that the herd had moved on. Most likely, Mike observed as he looked at the few reeds still growing beneath our trees, the elephants had to leave to find other food sources. The only hope Mike offered was that perhaps the herd would return in a year or two. Of course, the chance was slim that the timing of the herd's return would intersect with our visitation schedule. We therefore girded ourselves to the thought that we might never again see Our Elephant and her herd. Perhaps it was time to turn our attention to a different set of African experiences.

CHAPTER FOURTEEN

Humility Breeds Respect

And say my glory was I had such friends.
—William Butler Yeats

Chapter 14

To say that our African experiences focus solely on sitting with elephants is to misrepresent what we have done during our African winters. In fact, the interactions with the elephants are often the icing on the cake to our African visits. Much of our time in Africa is spent doing other things—seeing other animals, visiting other people, or quietly driving within the bush while reflecting on and being thankful for having the opportunity to visit this magnificent area.

Yet we never forget and always appreciate the fact that interacting with the elephants introduced us to the power of humility. This introduction taught us how a humble perspective reshapes the way we interpret events and interact with people. This humble perspective has, metaphorically, opened the door to let us experience other facets of Africa from a different perspective. We go to Africa each year not to criticize or even to suggest ways to improve. Nor do we go to convert. Instead, we go to watch, experience, and learn. It would be arrogant to do otherwise.

If someone asked us to define in one word how we have learned to approach Africa, the word we would choose is "respect." We strive to respect the African environment, the African animals, and the African people. And our personal definition of respect is that it is owed, not earned. We owe respect to the environment. The environment is a gift we were given and must preserve. We similarly owe respect to the animals. They, too, are a gift. I sincerely believe that many of these animals have the capacity to identify human respect. This tendency reveals itself when the animals elect to stay in your presence a bit longer than normal; at other times, animals acknowledge respect by leaving you alone.

Finally, and most importantly, humans are owed respect—those who live in not just in Africa or the United States but anywhere. Stated simply, the minute you meet someone, you owe that person respect. If you walk into a room filled with people, you owe respect to each and every person in that room. No one should have to earn your respect. Expecting people to do so is a subtle form of arrogance. Instead, it is your obligation to bestow respect. People can, of course, lose your respect through the way they conduct themselves. Thus, giving respect is your obligation, but retaining respect is the responsibility of the recipient. But based on personal experience, I assure you that once people perceive you respect them, they will go to great lengths to preserve that respect. It is a gift we do not want to lose.

Humility and respect are closely intertwined. Humility is the foundation of respect. It is what respect is built on. Humble people respect others; arrogant people don't. Metaphorically, the arrogant spend all their time looking in the mirror, praising their accomplishments and ideas. The arrogant are unable to recognize the value of someone else's ideas. And when things go badly, the arrogant overlook their own contribution to the problem and promptly blame others for the undesirable outcome.

Humble people turn away from the mirror. In doing so, they often see people doing their best to persevere and do the right thing under implausibly difficult conditions. Often, these people have wonderful stories that need to be heard. All we have to do is listen.

The staff at Sabie Park and the Protea Hotel have shared hundreds of stories with us over the decade we have been in Africa. The tellers share these stories only after recognizing the deep respect we have for them. Consequently, the stories come from the heart, not the head. The stories are not trying to promote a particular point of view; nor are they trying to convince us to believe anything or act in a certain way. Instead, the stories demonstrate a bond between the teller and the listener. In this process, the teller forges an understanding with the listener as to why the storyteller is who he or she is.

Some of our favorite stories come from Elsie, a Protea employee who works in the restaurant. She is one of the many staff members who come to visit while I'm connecting to the internet in the television room. Elsie has two children. One is her biological daughter; the other was adopted after Elsie's sister died.

Dear Dan and Laura,

A quick note from the Protea television room.

Elsie, one of my favorite people at the Protea, brought me coffee a few minutes ago, and we had a wonderful chat. The impetus for the conversation occurred when I asked her about working at the Protea. She said she likes her job a lot and added that she has done it for over twenty years. She then added that she once left for another job, but it didn't work out. I asked her for details, and she shared the following story.

Elsie's other job involved working as a nanny for what she labeled "a white family." The family had two young children. Elsie's charge was to raise them properly.

I asked Elsie what happened to the nanny job. She said that she quit right before the family was going to fire her. I asked why she was going to be let go, and she said, "I couldn't control the children." That was difficult to believe. Elsie has a presence that would make any adult, much less a child, do whatever she wanted. She is dignified and confident, and carries herself with pride. She is also highly intelligent, and she knows that.

I shared the above observations with Elsie, being sure to pose each characteristic as a compliment. Then I added, "It is impossible to believe that you couldn't control anyone's children."

Elsie's reply was classic: "It's impossible to control a child when that child's parents don't respect you."

Elsie then continued: "The children's father and mother treated me like a servant. They ordered me around and constantly told me what to do. 'Get this!' 'Clean that.' 'Never do that.' Even worse, they treated me this way in front of their children."

The children, being children, did what children do—they imitated their parents' behavior. "The children would give me orders rather than obey me," Elsie continued. "When I told tell them to do certain things or to behave in certain ways, they would simply say, 'No.' It was terrible."

Elsie then added that the parents could never understand why she couldn't control the children. They never saw the example they were setting.

A fierce pride burned in Elsie's eyes as she told her story. The pain of the experience still hurt, even though it had been more than five years since the event occurred.

Elsie then shifted the conversation to a more upbeat note. She said that she really appreciated that the Protea management gave her the opportunity to return to her job. She tried something else, it didn't work, and the Protea gave her back her job. "I will never leave the Protea again," Elsie concluded.

Perhaps that family failed to respect Elsie, but the Protea management recognized a valuable person. They welcomed her back with open arms.

I hope you folks are well.

Love,
Dad, the Avid Listener

We all need to remember the important lesson here. Respect and lack of respect are contagious. When we treat someone with respect, that person is apt to treat us with respect. Others, in turn, recognize and imitate our respectful behavior. On the other hand, as the children in Elsie's story demonstrate, when we disrespect another person, we not only hurt our relationship with that person but we influence the perspectives others have about that person as well. Hence, disrespect can spread like a contagion. And contagions are never healthy.

An area of respect that people need to be especially careful about when traveling internationally is their perceptions about topics, trends, and aspects of life that are different from those to which they are accustomed. Foods are different, but that does not mean they are not tasty, if you open your mind to eating seaweed, crabs, or eel. Likewise, names sometimes seem unusual to people from different cultures. In South Africa, for instance, the hood of the car is called the "bonnet," while the trunk is called the "boot." These names sound unusual to an American, although they are quite normal for anyone from England. And, once you become accustomed to the names, they seem appropriately descriptive.

People's names are a unique and particularly surprising feature to first-time visitors to Africa. The names, especially when translated into English, often sound unusual to those not raised in the area.

Often, the names are more descriptive than a Westerner is accustomed to hearing. Some of the great names of the Protea employees include: Forget, Curious, Surprise, Wonderful, Happy, and Beautiful. Each name conveys the feeling the parents had at birth. We have met hundreds of Africans who wear their names with pride, respect, and dignity. Hence, although these names at first sound strange to a Westerner, it is imperative that we recognize and honor the names people carry.

We also encounter a compendium of interesting names when we drive to Hazyview, especially when we park at the Pic 'n' Pay grocery store. Parking here involves an important ritual that is repeated in various places throughout Africa. Essentially, you don't just park and walk away; instead, you park and then hire someone to guard your car.

The process of hiring a car guard is ritualistic. Young men and women walk around in the parking lot, guiding you to spaces for which they are responsible. Once you park in an area, the guard controlling the area approaches you and offers to "watch" your car. If you want the guard's services, which most people do, then you say, "Yes, please do so." You then follow that request with a question: "And what is your name?" The young person will offer his or her name to you. Sometimes the name is already on a nametag.

This ritual has led us to discover an array of wonderful African names. Again, at first these names seem unusual, but over time we have not just become accustomed to these names; we have learned to treat the names and the holders of the names with respect. The names of the young people who have guarded our car at the Hazyview Pic 'n' Pay include: Mistake, Blessed, Bubble, Quick, Sunshine, Cloudy, and Rain.

But our two favorite names among these car guards are Nobody and Somebody. We do not know if they are related to one another or if the name oppositions are coincidental. However, it is fun to think of a rendition of the famous Abbott and Lou Costello scenario whenever one of these two protect the car. Here is a brief, adapted version of the skit:

> Sally asks who is guarding the car in the parking lot. I reply, "Nobody."
> She replies, "Shouldn't Somebody guard the car?"
> "No," I reply, "Nobody is watching the car."
> "Well, Somebody should . . ."
> And the conversation continues.

The name that I appreciate most of all is Mbkaphi. Mbkaphi is a Protea employee who occasionally serves coffee in the morning when I am using the internet. He is, by the way, the only Protea employee who uses the Tsonga name on his nametag. All the others use English translations.

Dear Dan and Laura,

Mbkaphi is a middle-aged man who moves with a noticeable limp. He is mobile, but it's obvious that moving for him is a bit of a chore. He never complains and is actually one of the fastest employees at the Protea in terms of accomplishing his tasks. He is also a bit shy and reclusive. He hides these tendencies through a highly formal and proper approach. "Distinguished" would be an appropriate word to describe Mbkaphi. He seldom smiles since it might undercut his professional demeanor. However, on the occasions when he does smile, he lights up the Protea's veranda.

One morning Mbkaphi and I were chatting in the television room. The conversation was free-flowing and extremely relaxed, so I took the opportunity to ask about his name. Specifically, I asked for the English translation. Mbkaphi paused, looked at me with appreciation, and said that it translates literally as "Where Can I Hide." The preferred English translation is "Hidden."

Mbkaphi then asked if I wanted to know the reason behind the name. I said, "Yes, please." So he continued.

When he was born, he said, his mother looked at him and instantly noticed the deformity of his right foot. At that moment, she instantly knew what he had to be named.

She chose Mbkaphi because he had to be protected; he had to be kept away from others; he had to be "hidden." "Remember," Mbkaphi continued, "in the bush, animals that are deformed are either abandoned or killed.

"My mother," he added proudly, "chose to protect me."

He had a look of sincere appreciation in his eyes. Then he thoughtfully added, "She did a good job."

I hope you folks are well.

Dad, a Name of Which I'm Proud

Finally, on this topic of names, I acknowledge with a mixture of pride and humility that I have my own African name. I am

Nkhalamba ndi ndodo. Sabie Park staff bestowed the name on me. I learned about the name by accident, but it's a great name. I wear it with pride.

Hello Dan and Laura,

Just a quick note to let you know that I have a new name. It's . . . well, wait a minute; you need a little background to appreciate it. I won't drag this out too long, but you have to understand the context.

As you probably remember, I take a daily walk in Sabie Park. I go alone but take along an awesome stick that I found in the backyard. The stick is solid cane. It is a meter and a half long and twenty centimeters in circumference. All in all, a solid piece of wood.

The stick serves both as a walking cane and a form of protection in the event that I have an unfortunate encounter with a wild animal. The thought is that the stick will let me "bluff" a leopard or a lion for at least a few minutes. And if you're about to be eaten by something, then those few moments are precious.

Anyway, I walk with my stick daily along Sabie Park's dirt roads. The roads are hilly, so I frequently use the stick for support.

On most days I walk between five and eight kilometers—it takes an hour to an hour and a half to do so. Then, I come home, shower, rest, and try to recuperate before we take our late afternoon drive in the Kruger.

I walked today—uneventfully—and then we went for our Kruger drive. We had fabulous viewing in Kruger today, topped off with a view of a mother lion carrying a cub across a dirt road. She was moving the cub from a hiding place near the river to a more remote location in the park. The cub was very small. The mother was carrying the cub gently even though she had the cub by the back of its neck. The viewing occurred at 17:25, so it was too dark for pictures. And since the park closes at 17:30, we had to leave rather than "hang around" and hope for another viewing.

Needless to say, we were pumped after witnessing this scene. We were too excited to just go home and rest. So we decided to have dinner at the Protea.

We always say hi to the front desk staff as we walk past on the way to the restaurant; most of them know us as the "strange old Americans" who love Africa. However, the young lady who was working tonight was someone we had never previously seen. We said hi anyway.

She looked at us, smiled, and said hi as well. Then, like all front desk people around the world, she lowered her head and resumed staring at the computer screen in front of her. After a brief moment, however, she raised her head, looked directly at me, and said, "Hey, you're the man who goes for long walks in Sabie Park."

I smiled and said, "Yes, I am."

She then added that she had friends who worked in Sabie Park. She added that she and her friends had seen me walking there earlier today.

I smiled and said, "Yes, I had a good walk today."

She looked away and seemed ready to lower her head and resume staring at the computer screen again. But instead she stopped, again looked up, and asked if I knew that that staff at Sabie Park had a name for me. She was smiling warmly, and her brown eyes had that light-hearted, friendly twinkle so frequently seen in South Africans' eyes.

I said that I did not know that I had been named. She replied, "Yes, they call you 'Nkhalamba ndi ndodo.'" Her enunciation sounded guttural but rhythmic.

At this point, I couldn't resist and had to ask, "What does the name mean in English?"

She paused and smiled. She seemed to be debating whether she should translate the statement or not. Then, with an even larger smile and a brighter light in her eyes, she said, "It means 'Old Man with Big Stick.'"

I have no idea if she knew the compliment she was paying me!!! The smile and twinkling eyes told me she did. I can assure you Mom knew what I was thinking. As proof, she groaned, "Oh no." Mom instantly recognized that I would gladly adopt this name and that Mom would have to listen to this story for years to come.

What else can I say? I have an African name—and it certainly is, in my opinion, a great moniker.

I can't wait to get home to share my new name with our friends. I will be the envy of the bridge club.

I hope you guys are well.

Love,

OMWBS

PS: Let me know if you need me to interpret these initials. I will be happy to do so.

PPS: OMWBS—YESSSSSSSSSSSSSS!!!!!!!!!

The stories shared so far in this chapter convey, I hope, the deep affection, admiration, and respect we have for the African people with whom we interact. Yet it is important to add a qualifier to these relationships: the majority of the African people with whom we interact work in the service industry.

Many are employed at the Protea Hotel; others work at Sabie Park; some are employed in the Kruger. Each of these places has a service component. As a general rule, the service industry draws and retains those who are more outgoing and friendly. Hence, our African contacts are self-selected.

This means that African people with whom we interact on a daily basis are far different, or at least far less vocal, than are the members of some of the political parties in South Africa, including the Economic Freedom Fighters. This group, labeled the EFF, advocates nationalizing most industry in the country and the direct seizure of homes, property, and other assets held by South African whites. A little over 10 percent of the South African electorate supported the EFF in a 2016 nationwide election. Estimates are that more than 30 percent of South Africa's Black population identify with and support this party. To my knowledge, I have never met an EFF member. However, again, my contacts are self-selected.

Finally, and perhaps most importantly, our relationships with our South African friends are complicated by a host of external factors. Most are young or middle-aged—we are old, especially so by local standards. Most are Black—we are white. Most were born and raised in the immediate area and have never traveled more than thirty kilometers from home—we commute to South Africa annually from the United States.

But the most complicating factor of all about our relationships is that our friends work in professions that involve service fees. The acceptance of a tip would be a violation of ethical norms to an American university professor. No student has ever offered me a penny for teaching a good class. It just doesn't happen in my profession.

This difference is significant. This "tipping culture" means that many of the employees we meet are dependent on us for part of their modest income. We are large tippers by South African standards. Many people leave no tips at all. Others see the top of the scale here as 10 percent for excellent service. We are apt to tip in a range of 20, 30, or 40 percent without hesitation. We are not wealthy people; tips are just a modest way that we can help a bit.

This tipping issue is important to acknowledge not from a perspective of self-promotion (such a claim would contradict any efforts to improve in the area of humility), but from the perspective that it complicates being able to measure our personal relationship with the staff. Hence, while we consider many of these people as friends—in fact, I would contend that they are "good friends"—they most likely view us partially as friends but equally as a source of income.

Yet there is a joy and a reward to having friendships with a financial component. It feels good to know you are helping a friend. Evidence of this joy occurred one year when we were having a final lunch at the Protea prior to departing for the United States.

> Dear Dan and Laura,
>
> Just a quick note to record a touching "end of the year" experience. We leave for Johannesburg tomorrow morning and head home from there tomorrow evening.
>
> We said our goodbyes to the Protea staff yesterday. When appropriate and possible, I slipped a couple of one hundred rand notes to people we had not been able to offer tips to during the year. Richard, the porter, for instance, is one of my "talking buddies," but we never need his services. Hence we

never offer him any financial assistance during our visit. So when I saw him walking alone along the Protea walkway, I slipped him a two hundred rand note. He not only said thank you—he hugged me. A most meaningful gesture.

But I digress. That hug is not the important one in this email—another one is. Calvin, one of our favorite Protea friends and one with whom we have interacted frequently in the many years we have been here, was the server yesterday. Both of you have met Calvin. He is the razor-thin elderly man who, unfortunately, is not the picture of good health. But he is always cheerful, kind, and considerate. He also always seems genuinely happy to see us. I'd label him one of the best people we have ever met in the African bush.

I should add, by the way, that Calvin is frequently the recipient of many of our larger tips. Mom contends that these tips are one of the reasons Calvin is always happy to see us. I don't share her cynicism—at least not exactly. I think he genuinely cares for us, as we do for him. But these relationships are complicated.

But I stray from my point. Back to the event. Calvin delivered the food yesterday. When he did, I told him we would be leaving tomorrow to go back to the United States. Calvin looked concerned and confused. He then asked, "You will be back next year, right?"

I responded glibly, as I tend to do, with the following observation: "Calvin, we will be back next year and for as long as we are able to get to our house in Sabie Park. The day may come when we are so old that we can't get out of that house. But even then, if we can get to the bush, we'll still be here."

Then, without pausing, I added, "Calvin, if that day comes when we can't get out of our house, we will still want to see you. So I guess you will just have to walk to Sabie Park to bring us some food." I smiled as I made this statement and assumed Calvin would recognize the humor of the statement.

To my astonishment, Calvin took my statement seriously. He totally missed my intention of being glib. Instead, he replied in an extremely solemn tone: "It would be my honor to walk to your house to bring food to you."

The seriousness of Calvin's response took us aback. I looked at him but didn't know what to say. Calvin grabbed control of the moment and continued, "You have helped feed my family for the past seven years. I would walk to Sabie Park or any place you needed me if you had to be taken care of."

Tears filled my eyes. I looked at Mom and tears were flowing down her cheeks. We had both just experienced a very special moment. I stood up, as did Mom, and the three of us hugged. It was a moment that needed a hug. Calvin, by the way, was crying too.

I should add that our bill for lunch was 135 rand. I gave Calvin a 200 rand tip.

We look forward to seeing you in a few days.

I hope you folks are well.

Love,
Dad, the Huggable Tipper

Even though "tipping" complicates our relationships, I sincerely do not believe that I am buying the staff's affection. To assume that undercuts the sincerity of the relationship. I am the first to contend that I regard the staff at the Protea and at Sabie Park as friends. And when they call me "friend" as well, I think they do so with a similar level of authenticity. I trust in and value their friendship. Tips, therefore, are not really tips at all—they are gifts between friends. It's not about service; it's about friendship. And friends share what they have.

CHAPTER FIFTEEN

Changes in Latitude, Changes in Attitude

It's these changes in latitude, changes in attitude
Nothing remains quite the same.
—Jimmy Buffett

Only connect!
—E. M. Forster, *Howards End*

Humility is self-perpetuating. Stated simply, the humbler you become, the more you learn about other facets of life in which you need to be humbler. Some of these humbling influences come from watching the way life perpetuates itself in the African bush. It is nothing short of a miracle to watch a female dung beetle riding atop a ball of elephant droppings while the male pushes the ball to its destination. Awe translates to humility with the realization we have no such skills, nor do we make a contribution to the environment that is as important as the one they make.

On other occasions, the self-perpetuating nature of humility confronts us with flaws in our own perspectives. On these occasions, humility insists that we stop seeing events from a personal, self-centered point of view. True humility combats narrow-mindedness and opens our minds to alternatives. The humble therefore always remember that what we know may not be correct. It's not fake news; it is just wrong, incomplete, or inaccurate. Oftentimes a humble approach helps us remember that we interpret information or experiences from our own narrow line of sight.

A truly humble perspective reminds us that what we know determines what we know. In other words, the knowledge we hold influences our views and perceptions while simultaneously shutting out information that contradicts what we believe we know. Christians see everything through a Christian lens. Buddhists see information through a Buddhist lens. Likewise, capitalists measure the world against their preconceived standards, while socialists and communists use their own standards. There is nothing wrong with using your personal perspective, but a humble heart reminds us that others not only have a right to their perspective but also have reasons for believing it. At the very least we ought to respect these alternative views. It is arrogant to do otherwise.

Living humbly in the African bush challenges many of our established perspectives. Things we thought we knew and ideas we held as entrenched get turned upside down daily. The result is change. This change is sometimes in our beliefs; more often, it is in our perspectives. Both become broader and more open to new ideas and concepts. Humility encourages this openness, while the openness simultaneously develops a deeper level of humility. It's complicated.

Of course, this capacity to see things differently might come just from the change in setting. Hence two months a year in Maui might accomplish the same objective. But, for us, the African bush does the job quite nicely.

An early but highly valuable lesson on perspective occurred near the end of one of our yearly visits to the bush house. Mike and Lynda Crosbie had come to visit before we headed back to the United States. As always, we were looking forward to their visit. We expected to learn even more about bush living from Mike and Lynda. More importantly, Mike had promised to introduce me to the basics of "birding," an activity about which I knew little but wanted to learn more. Mike had promised to show me the difference between a fork-tailed drongo and a bee-eater. Information such as that seemed well worth learning.

Dear Dan and Laura,

Mike and Lynda Crosbie arrived last night. We had a brief but pleasant conversation after their arrival. Everyone then went to sleep so that Mike and I could get up early and begin my lessons on birding. As soon as it got light, a little before 7:00 a.m., I headed out with Mike onto the back stoep to get the day started.

Mike has a flair for drama. Since he knew that I was going to watch him "bird," he brought all of his paraphernalia out to the back stoep: binoculars, books, cameras, cell phone, and iPad. Then, before we began, and most certainly to create an added touch of drama, he paused, polished his binoculars, cleaned his camera, and carefully checked all of his equipment. I was pacing behind him all of this time thinking, "Come on! Come on! Let's go! Let's get started! Let's label some birds!" But Mike never rushed. He wallowed in the scene, enjoying my impatience.

After what seemed like hours, but was probably only minutes, Mike removed his reading glasses, picked up his binoculars, slowly put them to his eyes, and began scanning the backyard for what I assumed were sightings of rare birds. In less than ten seconds, he locked onto something. I watched him carefully. Nothing was moving. His head, his hands, his binoculars—all were perfectly still. I was transfixed by the way he concentrated on whatever it was he saw. Then, he slowly lowered his binoculars, looked at me with wonder, and asked, "Did you know you have a dead baboon in your tree?"

The question stunned me. I stared at Mike for a few seconds. Then I looked in the direction Mike was pointing. There, spread along the highest branch of one of our tallest trees, was a dead baboon. Its front paws were clutched around the branch. Its back legs flapped loosely in the wind. The display was at least thirty meters above the ground. I just stared at it.

After a few minutes, I asked Mike what I should do. His response was precise and targeted. "Don't do anything," he said. Then he added, "You're leaving in a few days. Something will eat it while you're gone. It may stink for a bit, but that won't be your problem since you won't be here." A "do-nothing" solution is, of course, one of my favorites.

Unfortunately, Mom didn't agree with Mike's solution. Being, in my opinion, a bit finicky, she didn't want to return to the United States with a dead baboon hanging from a tree in our backyard. Lynda agreed with her. So, in the interest of family unity, I undertook the task of finding a way to remove the baboon from the tree.

At the outset, let me state that I had no intention of climbing the tree to knock down the baboon. First of all, I don't have a ladder. Second, even if we had one, it would not have reached that high into the tree. Third, well . . . you get the point. I was going to "hire out" this task.

I briefly considered finding a phone book and looking for a baboon removal service. But then I remembered that we don't have a phone. So, after some additional thought, I decided to seek outside help. That's what brought me to see Peter, a Sabie Park resident.

Peter and I are "talking buddies." I don't know him well, but everything I have seen so far indicates he is genuine, nice, and certainly helpful. He is also a "connector," one of those people who know who to contact to solve most problems.

I described the baboon dilemma to Peter, and he promised

to get someone to help. Thirty minutes later I heard the sound of a truck clanging down the driveway. Inside the truck was the head of security, Albert, and his assistant, Elvis. Help was on its way.

Albert surveyed the situation and observed, "We need a plan."

I said, "Yes, I know."

Albert continued to stroke his chin, stare at the baboon in the tree, and repeat, "We need a plan." He repeated this phrase three more times.

Finally, losing a bit of patience, I said, "Albert, back in the United States, I teach a course about business strategy. Business strategy is all about planning. Over the years I have learned that planning is easy; it's the execution that is difficult. How are we going to get the baboon down?"

The prodding caused Albert to move to the next step and reveal a solution: "I'm going to make Elvis climb the tree to get it down." Whatever worked was fine with me.

Albert walked over to Elvis and seemed to give him directions to get down the baboon's body. The conversation was in Tsonga, so I don't know exactly what was said. However, it was readily apparent when the exchange became heated. My guess is that the interaction went something like this:

Albert: "Elvis, go climb that tree and get the baboon down."

Elvis: "Are you crazy? I quit."

Albert: "You can't quit, I've given you an order."

Elvis: "You can't give me an order. I quit."

And so forth. Yet the conversation was much longer and more energized and animated than this synopsis can convey.

Eventually, Albert returned and said, "We need another plan. I'll be back." Then Albert and Elvis got back into their truck and went bouncing up the driveway.

Forty minutes later, the bumping and clanging sound of a truck coming down the driveway returned. Albert and Elvis emerged from their truck and had an extension ladder and a lengthy wooden pole. Albert's plan was that Elvis would climb the ladder, poke the dead baboon with the pole, and force it to fall to the other side of the tree. Apparently,

Elvis was willing to climb the tree so long as he had the pole to assist him.

In no time at all, the equipment was in place and Elvis started up the ladder. But the plan had a flaw. Remember, that baboon had been hanging there for quite some time. Rigor mortis had set in. Those front paws were clasped together more firmly than Albert, Elvis, or anyone else had ever considered.

Elvis poked and poked at the baboon until he tipped, as planned, toward the far side of the tree. But the body did not simply fall to the other side. Instead, with paws held firmly together, the baboon's body rocked back and forth beneath the branch. A silly rendition of that children's bedtime rhyme came to mind as the baboon swung back and forth over Elvis's head: "Rock-a-bye baboon, in the tree top / When the wind blows the cradle will . . ." Then, without warning, the paws separated and the baboon's body fell straight toward Elvis.

What happened next is the stuff from which legends are made. Everyone shouted simultaneously, "Look out, Elvis!!!" Fortunately, Elvis must have studied ballet in an earlier life. Because as the dead baboon came plummeting toward him, he grabbed the side of the ladder with his free hand and swung effortlessly away from the ladder's rungs. For a moment, for one brief, shining moment, Elvis floated effortlessly in midair. His only connection to the ground was the one hand that was holding the side of the ladder. To make the scene even more amazing, Elvis held the pole in his other hand. He was "defying gravity." The Flying Wallendas could not have done better. And while Elvis hung there in midair, the baboon's body slid straight down the ladder.

The baboon hit the ground with a thud. Elvis promptly returned to the rungs of the ladder, climbed down, and helped Albert bag it up. The twosome then threw the baboon package into the back of the truck, loaded their supplies, and headed up the driveway, clanging all the way. It was a sight to behold.

A few hours after witnessing this "falling baboon miracle,"

I went to find Peter to thank him for arranging the assistance and to explain what happened. Peter appreciated the courtesy and enjoyed hearing the outcome. As the conversation came to a close, and as the events of the day took their toll on my energy, I made the following parting comment to Peter: "Sometimes living in the bush is really difficult."

Rather than ignoring my observation, Peter chose to challenge it. "You have that wrong, Ron," Peter responded as I turned to walk away. I looked back at him in tired confusion.

"Your observation," Peter suggested, should be that "living in the bush is wonderfully difficult."

He continued with the lesson: "You choose to live here, Ron. No one makes you do that. Others don't have that choice. More importantly, how many people can say that they have had a dead baboon in their backyard? I doubt that many Africans can say that, much less anyone from the United States. Remember, Ron," Peter concluded, "living in the bush is wonderfully difficult."

Lesson learned. Peter changed my perspective from "Woe is me. I had a dead baboon in the tree in my backyard this morning," to "Hey, did you know that we had a dead baboon in the tree in our backyard this morning?" That's a significant change in perspective. Peter, and this entire day, taught me a lot.

I hope you folks are well.

Love,

Dad, Partner in Ron and Sally's Baboon Removal Service

PS: Just as an FYI. The baboon was apparently injured by a leopard. His front torso was sliced open. The consensus among Mike, Albert, and Elvis was that the baboon had probably been mortally wounded in a fight and climbed high in the tree to get away from the leopard. The basis for this interpretation is the way the front paws were clinging together. If the baboon had been killed and stored by the leopard—an act that leopards frequently do to keep scavengers away from their kill—the front paws would have been hanging loosely in the same way as the back paws.

PPS: An addendum. I didn't get the above email sent

> yesterday because I was unable to break free to send it. This morning, before I left to send this email, I checked beneath the tree. Leopard prints are all around the area. Apparently, the leopard came back during the night to check on the baboon. I'll bet he was surprised when he found the branch was empty. "Damn it," he probably thought, "I was certain that baboon was going to die!"

Peter's perspective on the baboon event is worth remembering. It's another way that we can "Squeeze the Juice." The challenges we face can be burdens with which we cope or unique events we cherish. The glass is either half empty or half full. A golf ball that lands in a divot is either a bad break or another chance to demonstrate your skills. All things considered, the latter perspective makes life a more enjoyable experience.

On other occasions, the lessons in humility that the African bush teaches have undercurrents far deeper than the baboon story's. As mentioned earlier, some of these experiences invite or even force you to reexamine fundamental beliefs. In fact, sometimes a humbling experience in the African bush makes you realize that the way you have looked at the world for thirty, fifty, or seventy years may be the polar opposite of the way others see it. And with true humility, you have to acknowledge the possibility that the other view has validity.

In 2011, my Alabama colleague Lonnie Strickland invited me to join him on a gratis consulting job in the province of KwaZulu-Natal. This province is located eight hundred kilometers south of Sabie Park. It takes nine hours to drive to this location since you have to either pass through or go around Eswatini, the aforementioned former Kingdom of Swaziland. Either route has roads that are at times barely passable.

The province of KwaZulu-Natal was founded in 1994, the year in which apartheid ended, through a merger of the Natal province with the Zulu Bantustan. Voortrekkers, or Boers, traditionally occupied Natal. The Zulu tribe historically lived in the Zulu Bantustan. The Zulu king still lives in the area.

KwaZulu-Natal is similar in size to the country of Portugal. The terrain ranges from flat coastal wetlands that border the Indian Ocean to the magnificent Drakensberg mountain peaks. Pietermaritzburg is the capital of the province; Durban is the largest city. The province is the second most populous in South Africa, following Gauteng, which contains the cities of Pretoria and Johannesburg.

The organization for which we were consulting was Ezemvelo KZN Wildlife. This group, hereafter referred to as eKZN, is a governmental conservation group located in the KwaZulu-Natal province. eKZN is responsible for a number of important South African locations, including two World Heritage Sites, uKhahlamba Drakensberg Park and iSimangaliso Wetland Park. eKZN is also responsible for Hluhluwe-iMfolozi Park, which contains and protects the tropical savannahs of Zululand.

The appeal of this gratis consulting assignment was the opportunity to visit an area we had not previously seen. An additional benefit was that we were to be given informational tours of conservation areas within the eKZN system. The leaders of these tours were eKZN experts within their respective fields.

One of these experts, David, taught me much about conservation but even more about the importance of taking a humble view of others' perspectives.

Dear Dan and Laura,

A quick update about the trip to KwaZulu-Natal. We are learning a lot about eKZN, conservation, and South Africa's Zulu heritage. This learning brings me to today's story—one of the most enlightening I've ever encountered.

We are now at a location called Hilltop. It is one of eKZN's premier resorts. Hilltop is located in Hluhluwe-iMfolozi Park, which is Africa's oldest game reserve. The area was once the private hunting grounds of King Shaka Zulu, arguably the most famous Zulu king. The park is large, 96,000 hectares, and is located 280 kilometers north of Durban. A fascinating tidbit about the park is that it has the largest population of white rhino in the world. It takes about 3.5 hours to drive here from Durban.

As part of our introduction/indoctrination to eKZN, we were given a private tour of the reserve yesterday morning. Our tour guide, David, was a highly educated, well-spoken naturalist who was also a native Zulu. The task assigned to him was to educate us about conservation and about Zulu beliefs. To the Zulu, these topics are one and the same. One of the core Zulu beliefs is that nature and spirit intersect. David emphasized that a lot.

In summary form, here is what we learned from David: Zulus believe that a god named Unkulunkulu created everything in the world. Unkulunkulu was originally a reed but later took on human form. Unkulunkulu taught the Zulu how to hunt and grow crops.

David additionally pointed out that family is extremely important to the Zulu. Ancestors are treated with reverence and play a vital role in Zulu spiritual life. Stated simply, Zulu's believe their ancestors can influence events on earth. Zulu's thus honor their ancestors not just out of love and respect but also for practical reasons. These ancestors can provide protection and ward off evil spirits. Zulus speak directly to the dead ancestors and ask them to serve as intermediaries to God.

David explained these precepts to us as he drove us deep into the bush. Soon, he stopped the game vehicle, got out, and cut off part of a reed. He brought the reed cutting back and showed us the hollow part of the plant. This plant has special meaning to the Zulu, David explained, since the spirit of the ancestors can reside in the hollow of the reed.

David then went on to explain that when a close relative dies, a remaining family member will go into the bush, find such a reed, and cut off a piece. The relative will then return and place the reed cutting either on top of the casket or directly on the body of the person who has passed. The dead person's spirit then passes into the hollow part of the cutting and remains there forever. Tradition calls for that cutting to be kept in a place of honor in the living person's house.

David then became even more personal. He explained with amazing solemnity how he had placed a cutting of this reed on his father's casket. He has since kept the cutting in a private room in his home. David said that he often goes into the room to discuss events with his father. He even seeks advice when necessary. David then added, continuing in a serious, almost sacred tone, that his father has never failed to provide insight and wisdom to whatever problem David is facing.

Dan and Laura, please note: some fathers don't have to die for their children to gain amazing insight and wisdom by talking with them. Perhaps just an occasional call?

Back to David. All in all, a most impressive story. I, of course, as you might guess, enjoyed hearing about the intersection of nature and spirit. However, even I, Mr. Nature/Spirit, thought that David's description of the connections may have been a bit overboard. However, since I really liked and respected David, I expressed no disagreement with his views.

Last night we were hosted at a private and very extravagant dinner at Hilltop. Many local dignitaries were there, as well as the titular head of eKZN, who is also a high-ranking and well-connected politician in the South African government. I was overjoyed to be seated toward the back of the table beside David.

The evening's discussion flowed freely and enjoyably. Wine was shared, but not to excess. Eventually, the discussions stopped being table-wide and became concentrated within the immediate areas in which people were sitting. I took this opportunity to talk further with David. He was, again, charming, intelligent, knowledgeable and, all in all, a most pleasant "chap" to sit beside.

As the evening progressed, and as barriers to conversation continued to dissolve, I decided to pose what I thought might be a difficult but hopefully not an insulting question to David. I prefaced the question with lots of praise about how much I liked and respected him, how much I was impressed by Zulu beliefs, and how much I was impressed by his obvious intelligence and education.

Then, I asked a preliminary question: "Can I ask what might be a difficult question without meaning to insult you?" I was not being superficial. I wanted permission to proceed.

He paused, thought for a moment, perhaps reflected on my compliments, and said, "Sure, you can ask whatever you desire."

I followed with a brief, equally dramatic pause. Then I continued: "I was impressed by your explanation about the reed. And I was especially impressed to learn that you brought the plant with your father's spirit into your home, hold it in a place of honor, and go there to consult with him.

"However," I asked, again pausing both for dramatic effect and because I was a bit frightened to pose the question, "do you literally believe that your father's spirit resides in that plant? Or is your belief more symbolic?"

David listened intently and sent no signals of being insulted. So I continued with an additional set of questions: "And do you really believe that your father answers your questions? Or is that, too, sort of symbolic? In other words, since you obviously knew and loved your father intensely, are you perhaps developing an answer along the direction of what you know he would have said?"

I again asked him to please not be insulted by my questions. Meanwhile, I silently complimented myself for not adding that what he had described was fascinating but a little far-fetched for an educated twenty-first-century African.

David looked at me with kindness but confidence. He was obviously not offended. Then, without hesitation, he replied with assurance, "Yes, I truly believe what I told you. I believe every bit of it. My belief is not symbolic."

A long, slightly uncomfortable silence followed. I couldn't think of anything else to say. David broke the silence by asking if he could counter with an equally difficult question for me.

I said, "Certainly."

Similar to my lead-in, he added a qualifier: "No offense? And I'm not asking this just because of what you just asked me."

I said, "I understand. That's fine. Ask away."

Calmly and confidently he then posed the following question to me: "Do you literally believe that your God was born of a virgin; was crucified, died, and buried; stayed in the ground three days; rose to heaven; and occasionally, at least for a while, came back to earth and visited people? Additionally, don't many of you pray to your God, asking Him to intervene in daily matters?"

I looked at him with a mixture of amazement and appreciation. I wanted to say yes, but his questions and his perspective so stunned me that I didn't answer. One thought was dominating my mind as I sat there in silence. It was, "Wow! Did I just learn something?"

After a moment, David filled in the silence: "It is easier for me to grasp a spiritual connection between human life and nature than it is for me to understand the conventional beliefs that Christians profess. It's probably because the beliefs with which you are raised, combined with the experiences you have in life, strongly influence what you literally believe." He placed a special emphasis on the word "literally." I was not insulted.

"I understand," I replied. Then I added that I had never thought of how unusual the Christian precepts must sound to one not raised with those beliefs.

"Precisely," David replied, "I was raised to believe in a connection between nature and spirit. I never heard of your beliefs until I was an adult. So I guess that is why they seem so strange to me, even to this day."

"I underwent the same experience this morning," I replied. "I had never learned about Zulu beliefs."

I then extended my hand and said, "Friends?"

He reached out, grasped my hand, gave me an African handshake, a huge smile, and repeated my statement: "Friends." We then lifted and touched our wine glasses together.

What a day. I hope you folks are well.

Love,
Dad, the Enlightened

It is an understatement to say that David taught me an important lesson. What he ultimately did was broaden my perspective about the possible connections between nature and spirit. Even more importantly, he gave me another African lesson in humility. As I reflected at length on our conversation, I came to realize that it is the ultimate act of arrogance to hold that one's belief system is superior to all others. This kind of arrogance has led to millions of deaths over the centuries.

Interactions with people such as David remind us that beliefs are just that—beliefs. They are not facts that can be proven or disproven. Humbly stated, they are "hopes" that we are right. It's important to have beliefs, but it is the ultimate act of arrogance to think that yours are superior to all others. Killing someone because of a belief does not change that belief into a fact. It's still a belief. If religions promote humility among their followers, then they should also encourage their proponents to practice it.

CHAPTER SIXTEEN

Africa Is Hungry

If a lion could talk, we could not understand him.
—Ludwig Wittgenstein

Sometimes Africa and the African bush teach humility through embarrassment. Specifically, while we strive to remember the elephants' lessons and become more humble, we simultaneously become skilled at looking the other way and ignoring or forgetting another message that Africa drills through our head daily: Africa is hungry.

And whenever Africa has to remind us of that lesson, we should, by all rights, be embarrassed.

As mentioned earlier, abject poverty surrounds you constantly in Africa. It is so pervasive that you begin to block it from your thoughts. You learn not to notice that person walking ten kilometers a day just to fill a bucket with fresh water. You ignore the combis—Black taxi cabs—that drive along the highways packed with people going to jobs that pay less than ten rand—seventy-five cents—a day. You walk on rather than watch an impoverished man pull a paper plate from a garbage can and lick it to get the last remnant of discarded food remaining on it. You sometimes turn the other way when children chase after you begging for rand so that they can get something to eat. You know that if you offer them rand, hundreds of others will emerge from the shadows with similar pleas.

Yet while it is understandable why we develop defensive mechanisms to block an awareness of poverty, it is also important to never get too good at doing so. It is selfish and self-centered to do so. It is wrong not to try to help. Any effort to help is similar to going into a nuclear war with a popgun, but it is an effort that needs to be made. No one individual will ever solve Africa's poverty problem, but we must contribute when and how we can. Most importantly, we must never forget the humbling lesson that Africa constantly teaches: "Africa is hungry!"

One of the most poignant reminders of this message occurred one morning while I was driving to the Protea Hotel to use the internet. To enter the Protea grounds, visitors first have to pass through a guarded gate. Over time, I have become friends with many of the gate guards. We usually exchange pleasantries while I fill out the appropriate forms to enter.

> Dear Dan and Laura,
>
> Good morning from the television room at the Protea Hotel. I drove here a while ago to have a cup of coffee and use the internet. I always wave at the staff in the restaurant as I walk into the television room. Then, a few minutes later, one of the staff, usually Elsie, Calvin, Mbkaphi, or Alec, appears in the room with a pot of coffee for me.

The conversation that follows begins in a ritualistic manner. It goes as follows:

"How are you today, Professor?"

"I am fine. And how are you?"

"I am wonderful, Professor."

Often the hotel is busy, so I'll pay for the coffee—and include a generous tip—and the server will be on his or her way back to the restaurant. If things are quiet at the hotel, or if I pick up a nonverbal signal that the staff member would like to talk, then I try to ask them about their lives. You know from earlier emails that as the staff has gotten to know me, they have become open about their challenges, troubles, hopes, dreams, family encounters, and so forth. I am appreciative whenever they are willing to share a part of their lives with me. The interest that I express is genuine.

Over time I have also become "talking" friends with the gate guards. Both Sabie Park and the Protea have gates that you pass through in order to enter the location. It is sometimes difficult to converse with the Protea guards because of language problems, but each always smiles and with some I have a stilted conversation.

Today at the Protea gate I had a most humiliating experience. A female guard, Blessing, was on assignment. Blessing's skills in English are the best of any of the Protea guards. She is one of my favorites. Blessing has sparkling eyes, a room-lighting smile, and that shiny skin that God gave to so many Africans. Based on appearance, Blessing is appropriately named.

I should add, before I tell this brief story, that Mom and I occasionally go to the Protea for breakfast. However, I never have breakfast alone—only when Mom is with me. Of course, none of the gate guards know that.

So I drove alone to the Protea this morning and Blessing brought, as she always does, the clipboard that I have to sign before entering the Protea grounds. In an effort to begin a conversation, she asked if I was going to the hotel for breakfast or just to have coffee. I noticed as she asked the question that she was scanning the car with those gorgeous brown eyes. She focused particularly on the leftover food, the candy wrappers, the drink bottles, and other paraphernalia that accumulates in the car while we are out watching animals.

Guards and anyone else in Africa scan the insides of the car whenever you are stopped. The process is amazingly efficient. On occasion the scanner will allude to an item present. In my case, it is often the laptop that sits on the seat beside me. Although I don't believe any of our friends would do so, I cannot help but consider that the car's contents are being surveyed for potential thievery. Again, I don't believe any of the friends who know us would do that to us. So perhaps, at least in our case, the "scan" is just a habit. But make no mistake, things do disappear from cars whose doors are left unlocked or windows open. Stealing is rampant.

My response to Blessing's inquiry about having breakfast was a gentle laugh, a friendly smile, and a cordial response that I was going in just for coffee, not breakfast. I continued the conversation by adding, "We had too much to eat here last night. I don't need more this morning."

Then, in an effort to seem self-deprecating, and hoping to interject a bit of levity into the conversation, I patted my stomach, which was extending far over the seatbelt, and added, "This is large enough already. I don't need to be filling it further with a big Protea breakfast." Finally, in closing, I added, "No. I'm not hungry."

I looked in Blessing's face to see if she enjoyed my humor. To my astonishment, Blessing's face looked somber. Her sparkling eyes had dulled. A pall came over the setting. Blessing then looked straight into my eyes and, without remorse or even a hint of wanting sympathy, said, "I am always hungry."

I was stunned. I didn't know what to say. My insensitivity embarrassed me. I did not know what to say, so I replied with a simple but sincere, "I'm sorry." Then I drove through the gate and entered the hotel grounds.

Now I'm sitting in the television room thinking about what happened. What a terrible situation. You want to know one reason people steal in Africa? It's because they are hungry.

They take something from your car or your house to trade it for food. Who am I to judge this action? I would do it too if I were that hungry. And I'm even more certain that I would do it if either of you were starving. What other alternatives are available in a country that has an actual unemployment rate of over 50 percent?

So I am sitting here in the television room, wondering what I should have done. Given her money? Perhaps. But she wasn't asking for that. She was just telling me the truth. And if I had given her money, she would then tell other Protea guards, and soon everyone would be sharing their hunger stories. Of course, these stories are true too. They are probably truer than the stories I hear from family and friends. But I choose—and the world chooses—not to hear these stories.

So we make excuses. "You can't feed all of them" is a stock mantra that I hear so often. Or, as I do, we point out what we already do to help other individuals. I tip the Protea staff far beyond what is normal. And I give the guards at Sabie Park money when we leave. And I help the Sabie Park staff by . . . but these are just excuses. I am able and need to do more.

Damn, I wish Blessing wasn't hungry. Hunger is not a blessing. I wish that Africa wasn't hungry. But I don't know how to fix it. I'm not sure anyone does. So I drove onto the hotel grounds with my "belly" hanging out over the seatbelt. Sometimes, as a human being, I suck.

I hope you folks are well—I'm not.

Love,
Dad, the Guilt-Ridden

For years I had watched television announcements and read online advertisements about people being hungry in various parts of the world. Here I encountered someone who really was hungry but did not know what to do. It made me wonder about all of my African friends. I wondered how many of them are constantly hungry but are unwilling to share that information with me. Hunger is not a blessing. I resolved to increase my tips immediately—and resolved to broaden the range in which I provided tips. It is not a solution, but it made me feel a little less guilty.

A few weeks after this incident with Blessing, Sally and I were packing, cleaning our bush house, and preparing to make our end-of-the-season trek back to the United States. I was, as I had determined to do, providing cash gifts of appreciation to as many Sabie Park employees as possible. One of those recipients was Shaddrick, the manager of the Sabie Park supply store.

> Dear Dan and Laura,
>
> Just a quick note to document what I know but can never be reminded of too often.
>
> Earlier today I went to buy wood at the Sabie Park store. It's a little convenience store that sells a limited number of supplies. Shaddrick runs the place. He is extremely friendly and also delivers propane gas when we need it.
>
> I told Shaddrick that we were leaving tomorrow and, as is my custom, slipped him a hundred rand note in appreciation of his services and to help him out just a bit. One point of "tipping protocol." Shaddrick gets numerous tips during our visit. Actions such as delivering propane gas, fixing our refrigerator, and correcting the heat on our geysers, which are South African water heaters, lead to frequent fifty and hundred rand bequests. His departure gift is therefore smaller than those given to others. The guards at the Sabie Park gate get no tips during our visit, so we plant four hundred to five hundred rand on each when we leave.
>
> Shaddrick appreciated the hundred rand note and wished us well on our trip. Then, as I headed toward the door, he asked if I would do him a favor. "Sure," I said. "I will if I can."
>
> "Bring us any leftover food that you have? Don't throw anything away."
>
> "I will," I replied.
>
> "Thanks," he said. Then he added, "It is never pleasant going through garbage to find the food that's been thrown away." Finally, he added one more observation: "Often, I miss out on these leftovers because others get there ahead of me."

Damn, what a place. Africa is always hungry.
I hope you folks are well.

Love,
Dad, the Despondent

Shaddrick's comment hit me in the head like a hammer. Here I was cavalierly discarding leftover food that others wanted to eat. I had selfishly forgotten that when you are hungry, food, not money, is the immediate solution. I was giving my friends rand but throwing away food they desperately desired. The elephants may have introduced me to humility, but I still had much to learn about how to behave humbly.

Striving to take a humble view of life makes you aware of embarrassing contradictions. The interactions with Blessing and Shaddrick were both classic examples of blatant self-centeredness. I was seeing their lives through my lens, not theirs. As a result, I patted my stomach and threw away food with no recognition that they would see these gestures and actions from an entirely different perspective.

Sometimes fate wants to make sure you don't miss a lesson in humility. She therefore provided one additional reminder to me of the importance of a humble perspective. This lesson occurred in the Johannesburg airport as we were preparing to go home. This lesson showed me that life's contradictions are readily observable to those adopting a humble viewpoint.

Sally and I had driven from Sabie Park to Johannesburg earlier in the day. The trip usually takes five to six hours, depending on traffic.

Dear Dan and Laura,

Africa keeps teaching. When I don't learn the lesson, or forget what I've been taught, it reminds me again and again. I guess I'm a slow learner; on the other hand, sometimes when I do learn a lesson, I have problems remembering it soon thereafter. Fortunately, Africa perseveres in its effort to educate me.

Right now we are in the Air France's Sky Club in O.R. Tambo Airport. Pounds of meat, vegetables, and assorted other "goodies" are available for the taking. There is no charge for anything so long as you are a member of the Sky Club.

Lots of people overfill their plates and simply walk away from the leftovers when their flight is called. A barrage of waiters ambles about the room, removing half-filled plates. There is also lots of free alcohol. Interestingly, people always finish their drinks before they leave but walk away from the food. I guess they have their priorities straight (read that last sentence ironically).

Earlier today we drove from Sabie Park to Johannesburg. The drive was uneventful. We had lots of leftovers at the house, so we gave away most but brought along ample amounts to munch on during the trip. We even brought a disposable cooler so that we could tote cheese, milk, and other perishables. We dined pleasantly throughout the drive.

We arrived at the Johannesburg airport two hours ago. The Johannesburg airport is, to say the least, hectic. You have to be careful with your "stuff." We returned the rental car and loaded our belongings onto two carts. A trove of young men descended on us en mass as we walked away from the rental car agency. Two elderly white people pushing a loaded cart look like easy bait to this crew. I managed to fend them off with a forceful "we are fine; leave us alone" statement. And, of course, when they tried to engage us in conversation, we refused to talk and walked away. There are times in Africa when you have to be firm.

I started pushing one of the carts toward the check-in gate while Mom followed behind me with the other cart. We had not eaten much of the food that we brought, so I threw half a liter of milk, some cheese, and lots of other snacks into a nearby trash can. I left the disposable cooler to the side of the trash can so that anyone who wanted it could take it.

These people who bother you by offering to help are one of the more frustrating parts of the Johannesburg airport. The groups are composed of young men who want to push your cart, lift your bags, and so on. They are very aggressive. If you are at all hesitant or exhibit even a modicum of friendliness, they will begin helping you whether you want it or not. Signs throughout the airport tell you not to let these people help you; additionally, frequent announcements are made over the public address system telling you to avoid these young men. Superficially, of course, these young men want tips; however, the bigger risk is that some or all of your belongings may be stolen. The signs and announcements don't reveal this risk; they just say that you should only allow "uniformed agents" to assist. These "freelancers" have no uniforms.

Soon after I threw the aforementioned leftovers into the trash can, I heard footsteps from behind, turned, and saw a young male freelancer approaching. I increased my grip on the cart and turned to check on Mom. Quickly, my body position changed into a stiff, upright position. I was trying to look big, just as one does in the bush when confronted by a predator. I even stuck out my chest, which caused me to look a bit like a ravenous male baboon. In short, I was doing everything in my power to look tough and scare the freelancer away.

But the young man continued to approach. So I took the next avoidance step and started waving him off with a "no-no-get-away" gesture. The tough baboon had now transitioned into a waving circus chimpanzee. The young man continued to ignore my gesture and came closer.

As he started to talk, I said, "Get away from us. We're fine. We know what we're doing." But he looked at us with a different, less aggressive air. He came to within two meters and asked, "Was that milk you just threw away good?"

I said, "Yes, it was fresh. We drank some earlier today."

He then turned and began heading for the trash can. As he started walking, I called after him and added, "Hey, there is some good cheese in there as well. And some other snacks."

He said, "Thanks" and proceeded to stick his head into the trash receptacle to look around inside. Soon he pulled out his head and inserted his arm to remove the milk, cheese, and other assorted snacks. Then, he dumped the remainder of the trash can on the floor, sorted through what was there, and returned what he didn't need back into the trash. He eventually turned the receptacle back into an upright position.

We walked on and checked in our bags at Delta. But for some reason, I just wanted to see what happened. So I asked Mom to wait in a nearby store, and I returned to where the young man had been. The young man, along with three other "freelancers," was sitting on a nearby bench, feasting on our discards. The milk was being passed back and forth, the cheese was broken into pieces and shared, and the bags of snacks were evenly distributed among the group.

The young man saw me when I walked back. He remained seated, but his face broke into a huge smile. "Thanks, man," he said. "This is great!."

Again, it was another African "wow" moment. Our discards were satisfying a group of young men whom I had previously viewed as a bother. These people were hungry human beings, not bothersome thieves. It also didn't escape me that these young men never asked us to share food when we were holding it. But they were watchful as to when and where we discarded it. Hence they didn't beg for it. Of course, if you are as hungry as they are, you probably don't care how you get the food. You just want to get it.

Finally, I have to admit that my perspective on what these young men do in trying to help with travelers' bags changed dramatically. Suddenly, I recognized that they were not just hustling bags for money; they were trying to make a living, feed themselves, perhaps help others, and so on. Granted, what they do is against the airport rules, but what else can you do when you are hungry and there are no jobs available?

Now, here is the really bad part—a confession, as it were. I often give away full packets of leftover food when we leave but have been hesitant to give away items that are already opened. I have thus historically discarded partially used bags of corn flakes, half-used containers of oatmeal, crackers, and so on. It felt as if we were saying, "We have a lot, so we'll just give you the worst leftovers that we didn't eat." That seemed insulting. I forgot—or, more accurately, never thought about—that your threshold level for being insulted is really low when you are hungry. I should have given them all the food instead of throwing part away. Damn, that was just wrong. I hope I remember this lesson.

Enough.

I hope you folks are well.

I remain,
Dad, the Embarrassed

Even as I review these emails today, years after initially writing some of them, my insensitivity to the plight of the people around me is shocking. It is another "Africa-humbles moment." My earlier experiences with Blessing and Shaddrick had sensitized me to the hunger that pervades rural Africa. I failed to realize that similar conditions haunt those who live in the larger cities. Our discards were now satisfying a group of young men I had previously viewed as bothersome. And it is with a touch of humility and loads of embarrassment that I remind readers that the Air France Sky Club is less than two hundred meters away from where these young freelancers sought to be of assistance. So while the wealthy are walking away from half-filled plates to catch a flight home, these folks are tipping over trash cans to get the tiniest tidbit of discarded food.

I must additionally add, with some sadness, that these young hustlers are no longer a part of the Johannesburg airport's environment. About five years ago they disappeared. Now, only "officials" wearing distinct uniforms can help travelers in need. I wonder what happened to the young men.

Africa is hungry. We have on multiple occasions witnessed people in Johannesburg, Durban, and Cape Town going through garbage cans to find the smallest discards. On other occasions I have witnessed people actually remove plastic forks and cans of food and lick them to pick up the slightest of remains. Seeing people do that hurts.

Yet noticing the problem doesn't mean that you know how to solve it. I certainly don't. Solutions, if they come at all, will probably come incrementally. They will definitely involve political will, economic changes, and educational adjustments.

A few years ago, one of the guards at the Sabie Park gate, Lawrence, showed me a newspaper article published in the *Sunday Times*. The article entitled "Seven Crippling Beliefs That Are Keeping South Africans Poor" was a summation of the advice that Robert Kiyosaki, the author of *Rich Dad Poor Dad*, planned to present at the National Achievers Congress in Pretoria. Lawrence wanted to know if I knew Mr. Kiyosaki. We were, after all, both from the United States.

I said, "No, I have never had the honor of meeting Mr. Kiyosaki."

Then I looked at the article. Mr. Kiyosaki had flown in for a few days and was promoting his book's seven-step process as a solution for South Africa's problem. The underlying premise is that people should get a job, stay out of debt, avoid bankruptcy, and reconsider getting a higher education. Instead of going to school, Mr. Kiyosaki suggests that people should just work hard and be entrepreneurial. Mr. Kiyosaki probably flew home or to another speaking engagement as soon as the check that reimbursed him for speaking cleared. I wonder if his advice would help Blessing, Shaddrick, or the young men who went trash-can diving in the Johannesburg airport. I also wonder if Mr. Kiyosaki ever taught a lion to speak. I'm sure he could understand the lion.

Again, as I mentioned earlier, Africa's economic problems are complex. It would contradict the theme of humility to say that I know the answer to the dilemma of Africa's poverty. But as people who have spent their lives in the educational arena, and as people who see education as the great equalizer, Sally and I can do one little thing to alleviate a small part of the situation. We therefore made the decision, even before beginning to write this book, to donate all royalties to an educational trust fund that we have established for the children of the Protea and the Sabie Park staff. We realize this contribution is a minuscule step in a marathon of problems, but at least it's a start. We hope that readers feel a shred of assistance by having contributed to this fund through the purchase of this book. And if Mr. Kiyosaki ever hears of this contribution, he is welcome to match the royalties from his fees.

CHAPTER SEVENTEEN

Synchronicity

I wander'd off by myself,
In the mystical moist night-air, and from time to time,
Look'd up in perfect silence at the stars.
—Walt Whitman, "When I Heard the Learn'd Astronomer"

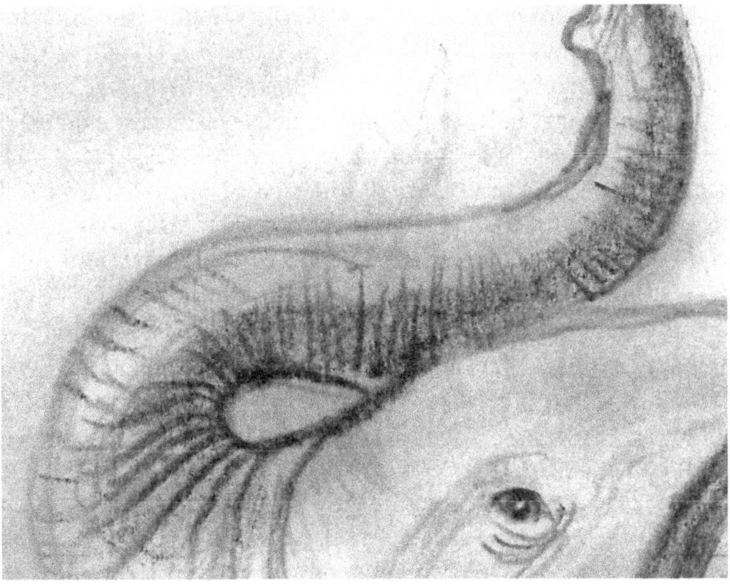

A final benefit of humility is that it makes us open to life's mysteries. In other words, once we admit we don't have all of the answers, we become capable of immersing ourselves in parts of life that seem unexplainable. We recognize that not all of life's answers can be found on an Excel spreadsheet. Even more importantly, we become comfortable with not knowing all of the answers. That, in turn, becomes part of life's pleasant mystery.

Synchronicity is a wonderful concept that becomes available once we take a humble approach and accept life's mysterious features. In its simplest form, synchronicity involves recognizing life's meaningful coincidences. On one level, these coincidences may be randomly related accidents. On another level, these coincidences may represent mysteries far beyond our understanding. I like to think of synchronicity as part of the poetry of life.

A few years ago my best friend from high school called to say "goodbye." He was in the last days of a terminal illness and wanted to express appreciation for our friendship. I talked to him on my cell phone while sitting in my car in a grocery store parking lot. After the conversation ended, and feeling a bit numb, I got out of the car with the intention of buying a few grocery items before going home. As I walked toward the grocery store, I noticed a beautiful rainbow looping over a nearby church. Oddly enough, the day was cloudy but not rainy. Yet the rainbow just arched there. That's synchronicity.

After noticing and enjoying the rainbow for a few minutes, I walked into the store. I finished my purchases and was walking back to the car with my head lowered. Thoughts of my friend were still foremost in my mind. Suddenly, in the middle of the parking lot, a stranger came up to me and asked if I had noticed the beautiful rainbow. She pointed toward the rainbow; it was the same one I had seen before but was now even prettier. Then, for reasons beyond understanding, she looked me in the eyes and said, "That rainbow is God's promise that everything will be okay." She then walked away without ever knowing the gravity of the conversation I had just completed ten minutes earlier. That's synchronicity on steroids.

The key events described in the remaining chapters occurred within a few days' span. For a literalist, the events are coincidental. For me, humbly, I believe they demonstrate synchronicity. There is more here than meets the eye. What seem like unrelated coincidences are, in my opinion, meaningful connections.

It was late July. Sally and I were having lunch at the Protea. It had now been more than a year since the elephants visited. To our delight, the server for the day was Elsie. However, in an uncharacteristic fashion, Elsie seemed rushed, almost rude. She handed us the menus and told us that we had to order quickly because she had to leave early. We complied. After a few minutes, Elsie returned to explain her behavior.

Dear Dan and Laura,

The morning began in an inconsequential manner: Lonnie Strickland had given Markus Hofmeyer, Kruger's head of Wildlife Conservation, a printer that I was supposed to get. Markus's office is in Skukuza, so I drove there to get it. I presumed the trip to Skukuza was going to be the highlight of the day. How wrong that was.

I picked up Mom after I got back from Skukuza, and we went for lunch at the Protea. We were excited to find that Elsie was going to be our server. We greeted her in the warm, friendly manner she deserved.

However, uncharacteristically, Elsie seemed rushed and disoriented. She took our orders quickly and curtly. I was a little taken aback by her brusqueness, but then noticed that she paused after walking away from the table. She then turned, walked back, and offered an explanation for her behavior. The bottom line was that she had to leave on time today—she often stays late—because she was going to funeral services for the daughter of another Protea employee, Johannes. Johannes is a pleasant middle-aged man who always stops to say "hi" while we are having lunch. We chat briefly and I find him a most enjoyable conversationalist. Given the opportunity, I suspect that Johannes and I would be very good friends.

We asked for more details and learned that Johannes's daughter was killed in a combi accident on Sunday. Combis are local taxis. Johannes had driven his daughter to Mbombela, a city formerly called Nelspruit. There his daughter was scheduled to catch a combi ride to Johannesburg, where she was attending college. Somewhere between Mbombela and Johannesburg, the combi rolled over. Other occupants were severely injured; Johannes's daughter was killed in the wreck. She was in her first year of college.

The story gets even sadder. Johannes has two daughters in college, both of whom attend school in Johannesburg. Both were originally scheduled to leave on Friday, but this daughter said that she wanted to spend more time with her family before leaving. So she stayed until Sunday, while her sister left on Friday. Johannes, Elsie said, had been extremely happy that his daughter wanted to spend more time at home. The other daughter made it safely to Johannesburg.

Elsie revealed that the staff was making a financial contribution to the family. Elsie's job was to take the contribution to the burial service. I asked Elsie if we could contribute, and she said, "Certainly." So I grabbed two hundred rand from my pocket and tossed the money into the pot. The staff thought it was generous; personally, I wish I had given a lot more.

Mom asked me a question after Elsie left to go into the kitchen: "Do you think Elsie could use a ride to the service?" I was actually wondering the same thing. Remember, transportation in South Africa is difficult. Few have cars. Mostly, people travel either by walking or by riding combis. But the combis are not always reliable, especially during off times or when you need to get to different locations.

When Elsie returned we asked if she needed a ride, and she said that it would really help. She added that others from the Protea planned to attend the service as well. In the end, we reach the following agreement: I will drive Mom back to Sabie Park and then return and take Elsie and other Protea staff to the services. As we left, I told Elsie that we could take five people if we used the seats in the back of the car.

So I took Mom home and then turned around and went right back to the Protea. When I arrived at the Protea's entrance, I saw Elsie with at least fifteen other people. Everyone had changed clothes and was "dressed to the nines." In the end I wound up with Rivers, the head server, sitting beside me in the front seat, while nine other Protea employees crammed into the back of the car. Four were in the back seat and five more crawled into the "way back" of the SUV. I don't know what happened to the other five staff members, but it was impossible to fit them in. I suspect they waited for a combi.

Now, don't miss this picture. Anyone looking at the road leading away from the Protea would see an SUV being driven by an elderly white man that was packed with ten well-dressed Black Protea employees. Nine of the employees were women; the tenth, Rivers, was a man. The people in the back two rows of that SUV were packed in like the proverbial can of sardines. But no one complained. Everyone seemed happy to be getting a ride. And it was readily apparent that the old white driver was not in charge. Everyone was telling him where to go. Ron and Sally's Combi business . . . we'll take you anywhere you tell us to go.

We left along the highway that separates the Protea from Sabie Park and headed toward Hazyview. Everyone turned silent once it was clear we were headed in the right direction. After we had gone about ten kilometers, Rivers pulled out a cell phone and said that he was going to call Johannes and tell him we were coming. He spoke to Johannes in Tsonga, so I couldn't understand the conversation. But he obviously went beyond just saying we are on our way. Specifically, he kept repeating, "The Professor; The Professor."

As an aside, I must add that no one at the Protea knows our given name. Everyone calls me "The Professor." Mom is called "Mrs. Prof." We hold these labels with honor. Based on Rivers's repeating of "The Professor; The Professor," I assumed he was telling Johannes that I was driving everyone to the event.

After another ten kilometers, Elsie told me to turn off the main road. She then guided me back into the township where Johannes and his family live. The dirt-path roads were filled with heavy sand.

I knew we had arrived when a tent packed with people came into view. The service had already started, with people singing what sounded to me like traditional African hymns. A man was leading the service, but the vast majority of the people under the tent were women. A group of men sat in an outside area beside the house about fifty meters from the tent.

I helped the women get out of the rear of the SUV and then started to get back into the car to leave. A few of the men and the women at the service were staring at us. I guess they had never seen a combi business run by an old white man. No one seemed threatening, but some looked confused. A group of about ten children—mostly between the ages of two and four years old—came running up, pulled at my pants, and said things that I didn't understand. Again, the situation was disorienting, but not threatening.

Elsie and Rivers stopped me before I could get back into the car to leave. Rivers said, "Johannes wants to see you." So I waited, and he came out of the house and headed straight to me. We hugged, and I told him how sorry I was. I also promised that we would pray for him and his family. He seemed to appreciate that. He also seemed to appreciate that I had transported the staff to the service. For a moment I thought he was going to ask me to stay longer. I wasn't sure if I should do so or not. I kind of hoped he would ask. It seemed like an opportunity to make a statement about crossing racial divides. "A white American attending an African memorial service," I thought, "what a wonderful thing to be doing." The singers in the service had even paused while Johannes and I were talking. I wondered if they were waiting for me to join them. I also noticed that more and more people were staring at me during the pause.

Elsie walked away as Johannes and I were talking but kept an eye on me. She also noticed the dilemma that I was getting trapped in. It was obvious to her that I wasn't sure if I should stay or leave. She also noticed that I was becoming the center of attention for many of the people attending the service. These folks were obviously wondering, "What is that old white man doing here?"

Fortunately, after a few minutes, Elsie grabbed control of the situation. She walked decisively toward the location where Johannes and I were talking, took hold of my left arm, looked me in the eye, and said, "Professor, it's time for you to leave." I appreciated the clarity about what to do. I hugged Johannes once more, got into the car, and drove away.

A number of the small children chased the car as I left. I lost them after I got onto the dirt path that was on the other side of the heavy sand. The children stared as I drove away. I wondered if they had ever before seen an old white man. I'll bet they had never seen an old white man delivering ten finely dressed Protea employees.

All in all, quite a day.

Please keep Johannes and his family in your thoughts and prayers over the next few days.

I hope you folks are well.

Love,
Dad, Driver for Ron and Sally's Combi Service

It is necessary to pause and briefly analyze what happened at this event. It's another important lesson in humility. I drove the Protea staff to the services with the purest of intentions. Then, at Johannes's invitation, I stayed and talked. But subtly, very subtly, arrogance snuck in. I was the only white person at a Black funeral; additionally, I was the only American at a South African event. I was becoming the center of attention and enjoying it. I even egotistically thought that the people in the tent were waiting for me to join in. On reflection, I realized they were waiting for Johannes.

Arrogance and egoism are cunning enemies. They are like twins who work together flawlessly. I convinced myself that my presence had a purpose larger than was initially intended. I was not just driving people to a funeral service; I was not just standing beside and offering condolences to a friend; I was instead, I convinced myself, representing something bigger. I was symbolizing openness, a willingness to cross racial, global, and economic divides. Each of these thoughts was about me. Each ignored the real purpose of the event, which was to honor Johannes's daughter and to console Johannes's family.

Fortunately, Elsie recognized what was happening. Her well-advised direction, "Professor, it's time for you to leave," rescued the sanctity of the event. Elsie kept the focus where it should be: on Johannes and his family.

Only upon reflection did I realize what Elsie saw instantly. I never intended to "steal the show," but it was about to happen. In fact, the way that some people were paying attention proved it had already started. Even worse, I was enjoying the attention.

Arrogance sneaks in through even the slightest crack. We must remain ever vigilant. Fortunately, in this instance, Elsie sealed the crack and saved the day. She told me to leave. I did. I will forever appreciate her perceptiveness.

CHAPTER EIGHTEEN

Good Fences Make Good Neighbors

He will not go behind his father's saying,
And he likes having thought of it so well
He says again, "Good fences make good neighbors."
—Robert Frost, "Mending Wall"

I drove back from the funeral alone. Elsie told me that the people I had transported to the services lived nearby. Each could, therefore, walk to their homes. That seemed fine with me, especially since Elsie had instructed me to leave.

I pondered the day's events as the car twisted and turned its way down the driveway. The ruts and bumps guided the car along the route with little need for my attention. It was good that nature was providing this guidance system since the focus of my attention was on what had just happened. The events befuddled me. Why had Elsie told me to leave? Had I done something inappropriate? Was my presence not sending the right message? Arrogance hangs around in the mind for a very long time.

Then, as the car navigated the final sharp driveway turn, I glanced over the hood of the car and saw what looked like gray tree trunks in the nearby bush. I did not remember trees of this sort being in this location. I looked more carefully and realized that these were elephant legs, not tree trunks. Paying more attention, I instantly noticed that three elephants were standing no more than two meters to the side of the driveway. The herd had returned while I was at the funeral.

I hustled into the house to see if Sally was aware that the herd had come back. I found her sitting on the back stoep, carefully watching what was happening. The elephants had come through the Kruger, Sally said, and went straight toward the fence in a ditch that is beside our backyard. Elephants visit this location frequently, usually pausing to rest and enjoy the shade. This time, rather than stopping to rest, the elephants walked straight through the fence. I asked Sally if Our Elephant was in the group that broke the fence; she said that she had not seen her.

Dear Dan and Laura:

The herd is back. They arrived midafternoon. I was away on an errand, but Mom was on the back stoep watching as they came through the Kruger. Mom watched as the herd broke the fence, crossed into our yard, and then split up. Three elephants walked beside the house and went toward the driveway; I saw these three when I returned from the errand. The majority of the herd moved into the empty lot to the east of our bush house. This lot is filled with scrub brush, vines, trees, and some reeds. This is the lot that separates our house from other houses, as well as Sabie Park's picnic area. The sound of cracking reeds and breaking tree limbs indicated that the majority of the herd was still in this area.

The temptation to observe the situation in the lot was irresistible. I grabbed my walking stick, and with Mom's warning to "be careful" ringing in my ears, I jumped into the ditch separating our house from the empty lot. I climbed out of the ditch on the other side and instantly saw an elephant munching on the branch of a nearby tree. She was facing away from me, so she couldn't see me. I tried to see if she had Our Elephant's identifiable cut in her ear, but couldn't do so from behind. Her huge body was blocking part of my vision of her ears. The bush was too thick to approach from the side, and Mom's advice to "be careful" wisely kept me from coming up behind her. As I stood pondering the situation, the elephant began walking away toward the Sabie Park picnic grounds. Soon, all I could see was her butt, but an impressive butt it was.

Another female—who was standing beside two very young babies—noticed me, stuck out her ears, and then started pushing the babies away from me. She moved the babies in the same direction the other elephant was going.

It was too dangerous to follow the herd into the heavy bush. So I returned to the back stoep. Together, Mom and I sat there waiting and listening.

The herd continued to break branches and smash reeds, but the sounds were fading a bit, so we suspected the elephants were continuing to move away from our bush house. Then, suddenly, silence. The herd was out of earshot. Everything was silent except for the eerie call of an African fish eagle flying over the Kruger.

The noises resumed five minutes later. The herd had reversed course and was sauntering back toward the house. Three elephants appeared at the back of the house, beside our driveway, and munched away at our trees. Other elephants walked back into the Kruger through the ditch beside our house. By this point the fence separating Sabie Park from the Kruger was nothing but mangled strands. Wires were sticking out in various directions. Our Elephant was nowhere to be seen.

We sat on the back stoep for ten more minutes. By now most of the herd had crossed the fence and was milling about inside the Kruger. The main group was twenty meters from the mangled fence. Then, suddenly, we noticed movement thirty meters from the fence. The few reeds remaining in the area began bending and swaying as though a wind was pushing them in various directions. But there was no wind. We stared intently at the reeds and noticed that they were beginning to move in a coordinated manner. One set was going to the left; the other set was going to the right. It was similar to the way that a curtain opens on stage as a play begins. Then, suddenly, the star emerged: Our Elephant walked forth from the curtain of the reeds onto the open stage in front of our fence. I had an urge to applaud.

She looked beautiful as she took the stage. She gazed about as if to check out her surroundings and then looked in the direction of our house. She seemed to recognize where she was but gave no indication that she recognized us. She continued to move toward the other elephants that were milling about closer to our house. When she got to within about five meters of the fence, she stopped and looked where we were sitting on the back stoep. She raised her trunk in a "sniffing" fashion. I honestly believe she could tell that old friends were in the audience.

Elephants have limited vision, so I doubt that she could see us. However, they have great olfactory senses. As she sniffed the air, she gave off a look of recognition. It was similar to the warm feeling you get when you recognize an old friend. Mom and I both agreed that we felt honored to be in her presence.

Our Elephant continued walking forward slowly. She stepped over branches and other vegetation and seemed to know exactly where she was going. She stopped when she reached the spot where the fence used to be. The wires were still lying on the ground.

It was now my turn to move. So slowly, with eyes cast downward, I began the approach. There was no mock charge. I gradually lowered my body as I got closer and closer to her. She waited for my arrival. Two other adult elephants emerged from the reeds and walked behind Our Elephant while I was making my approach.

I sat down when I got to within four meters of the mangled fence. From that point on I moved forward through my now perfected butt-scoot. Our Elephant swung her trunk slowly but never moved her feet. She watched intently. Twice she lifted her trunk in a sniffing fashion. I stopped going forward when I got to within two meters of her. At this point in my approach, I admit, I was more eager than I was humble. The approach was thus a bit rushed since I wanted to get close to her after being apart for more than a year.

An elephant's eyes are located on the side of their massive heads in such a way that they see better to the side than they do to the front. I therefore positioned myself to her left so that I would be within her range of vision. Also, I wanted a few extra seconds of escape time should things go awry.

The thought of having the elephant touch me with its trunk passed through my mind. The fence being down made this option viable. But the presence of a four-ton animal standing nearby eliminated the appeal of that idea. I therefore dismissed the thought as too dangerous.

We remained two meters apart for three minutes. Both of us seemed a bit uneasy; it was similar to two friends meeting after a long absence. At first, you are excited to see the other and catch up. But then, once you have done so, you run out of things to talk about. Thus, after our three minutes together, Our Elephant turned away, walked to a nearby tree, and began breaking off branches and munching on the leaves. I was still to her side; she was still watching me.

Two babies emerged from the bush and walked up beside the other two elephants. All four of these elephants remained behind Our Elephant. I kept a cautious eye on this foursome. The "Never-Get-Between-a-Mother-and-Her-Baby" rule was now at the forefront of my mind.

A few more minutes passed and then Our Elephant turned and walked back to the mangled fence. She walked toward me but did not cross the wires that were on the ground. The two adult elephants fell in behind her; behind them came the two babies. The entire group was staying on the Kruger side of the mangled fence.

The team of elephants walked directly toward me until they were no more than one meter away. As she had done the previous year, Our Elephant turned and walked her family right in front of me. It was awe-inspiring but frightening. The mangled fence was lying there to demonstrate what could go wrong.

The small herd continued walking along the fence line after they went past me. They were walking away toward my left. The babies followed for ten meters and then turned right and disappeared into the bush. I presumed they went off to join other members of the herd. Our Elephant and the two adult elephants continued along the fence for another ten meters.

What happened next occurred quickly but seemed to happen in slow motion. It resembled that moment when you are driving a car and realize that you are about to crash into another vehicle. You know you are moving quickly, but time pauses as all of your cognitive powers focus on what is about to happen.

To my utter surprise, Our Elephant and her two followers turned toward Sabie Park instead of the Kruger. The threesome thus stepped over the mangled fence and crossed into Sabie Park. They then turned left and began trotting toward me. It was definitely not a charge. But they definitely were coming toward me in a comparatively rapid manner.

I realized this was a defining moment in our relationship. The courageous side of my brain wanted to stay and see what would happen. It argued that we were about to have a once-in-a-lifetime experience. It was readily apparent that the elephants had no intention of harming me. This side of the brain therefore pleaded, "Stay here. You will have an experience like no one has ever had."

The cautious side of my brain jumped into gear as well. This side used visual cues to highlight the reality of the situation. Trotting toward me was twelve tons of elephant! Each elephant was at least ten feet tall. I am a slightly exaggerated 5 feet 8 inches tall. Plus, I'm old. The courageous side of my brain could argue, as it did, that these elephants merely wanted to play. But the cautious side observed that the elephants were not going to play gently.

The cautious side then ripped open my memory banks and reminded me of a newspaper article I had read two weeks earlier. An elephant killed one of three eKZN rangers in KwaZulu-Natal when the rangers accidentally scared a herd of elephants. The elephants charged, the rangers ran, and one accidentally tripped and fell. One of the charging elephants stopped, picked her up with his trunk, and threw her into a tree. She was dead by the time the other rangers reached her.

This cautious side of my brain delved further into my memory banks and pulled up readings I had done years earlier about people who try to raise lions from cubs. One danger of doing this is that the lion may ultimately become violent; a second, and greater danger, is that the lion may become too affectionate. Basically, the lion does a feline-like gesture of rubbing against you. No harm is meant. The gesture is done with affection. But the lion is strong and if it rubs against you in a restricted space, such as when you are against a wall, then there is a high probability that you will be crushed to death.

So, with a modicum of regret but a boatload of commonsense, I chose safety. I stood up and ran toward the house.

Again, I repeat, the elephants were trotting, not charging. But a trotting herd of elephants is still a sight to behold—especially when it is trotting toward you. So I hustled away. It might have been a once-in-a-lifetime experience if I had stayed, but then again, it might have been a once-in-a-lifetime experience because my life would have been over. I chose to live to sit another day.

Our Elephant stopped moving the moment I started toward the house. She looked disappointed. She then turned to her right and headed further into Sabie Park. The other two elephants followed. The elephants thrashed, gashed, and pulled at the trees outside our boma. A number of other elephants crossed the destroyed fence and joined them.

Eventually, after regaining my composure, I walked into the boma, leaned against the house, and took pictures. Our Elephant noticed me, extended her trunk over the cane fence that surrounds the boma, and began tugging on a tree inside the boma. She was pulling the tree toward the fence. She seemed intent on toppling the tree onto the fence. So with composure regained, and with thoughts of not wanting to have to pay to have the fence repaired, I walked to within two meters of her, waved my hands, and firmly shouted, "Don't do that."

She understood. She let go of the tree, turned, and walked further into Sabie Park. The other elephants stayed nearby for a while but eventually followed Our Elephant into Sabie Park.

What a day.

I hope you folks are well.

With love,
Dad, the Usain Bolt of Elephant-Sitting

Until the incident at the mangled fence, I had interpreted each of Our Elephant's actions from an optimistic, human perspective. We were, in my mind, friends. I firmly believed that I had the best of intentions for Our Elephant and that she had the same intentions for me. We were a team. These positive human interpretations continued even as she trotted toward me. Although I will never know why she chose to come forward, my primary thought even at that moment was that she wanted to get closer, perhaps to play together.

Previously I had wanted to be that close as well. But when the opportunity arose, I ran away. That move was literal and symbolic, as was the elephant's earlier crossing of the fence. At the crucial moment when I had a chance to bond with the elephant without a fence between us, I decided that we needed a barrier. From my perspective, she wanted to be closer than man and wild animal should be. So when I turned and ran to the house, I turned away not just from a four-ton elephant and her two four-ton friends; I also turned away from a belief that we could continue to be best friends forever.

This action redefined our relationship. It symbolized that we were never going to be as close as I had innocently hoped we could be. My actions tacitly acknowledged that we are two different species living in two different worlds. We could never become playmates. She is an African elephant. I am an elderly business professor.

Disney would have us walk off into the bush trunk in hand to live happily ever after. But that's a movie. In real life the bush is brutal and unforgiving. Mistakes happen. I was more likely to get hurt than I was to bond with a friend. The harm might not be intentional—I still believe that I was interpreting the friendliness of her actions correctly—but it was inevitable. So I left. She, in response, turned and walked deeper into the bush. Perhaps at that point she experienced a similar insight.

These running and turning events proved to be pivotal points in our relationship. Proof of the significance of these changes was to occur soon thereafter.

CHAPTER NINETEEN

A Trip to the Grocery Store and the Television Room

Where there's humility there is majesty; where there's weakness, there's might; where there is death, there's life. If you want to get these things don't disdain those.
—Saint Augustine

The day's events had taken a toll on Sally's and my nerves. We were too wired to sit in the house and relax. Yet we decided it was unwise to go outside and have a braai while a herd of wild African elephants tromped about nearby. So in an attempt to gain composure and a bit of normalcy, we decided to drive to Hazyview to buy groceries and experience a pleasant, relaxing meal. As so often happens in Africa, the trip provided a different perspective. It also demonstrated that if humility leads you to an acceptance of synchronicity, then an awareness of synchronicity may lead you to the realization that the gods, like the elephants, sometimes play Ping-Pong with you.

Hazyview, as previously mentioned, is a beehive of activity. Pic 'n' Pay, the local grocery store where we purchase supplies, is the queen bee of this activity. Employees, customers, suppliers, guards—the store is a tempest of action.

On most occasions, especially at the end of a long day such as the one we had just experienced, Sally prefers to wait in the car while I scoot through Pic 'n' Pay for supplies. I always hire a guard to watch the car while she awaits my return. On this occasion I hired Fabulous.

Dear Dan and Laura,

Just a quick note to share an incident that occurred earlier this evening.

Mom and I did a late afternoon run to Pick 'n' Pay, and as I was leaving the store, I noticed there was no line at the local Nedbank ATM. That is unusual. Plus, we needed some money. So Fabulous, our car guard, and I loaded the groceries into the car, and then I told Mom I was going to use the ATM. We explained our intentions to Fabulous, relocked the car, and I headed to the ATM. It was already dark, so I knew that caution was paramount.

The ATM had three machines, and only one was being used. A few people were milling around nearby, but that is par for the course. In fact, it is rare when only a few people are near the ATMs, so that made the situation even more advantageous.

All in all—as I've thought about what happened next—I think it was a rather professional scam. Nedbank's three ATMs are beside one another. A man was using the middle machine, so I went to the one on his right. This ATM was the closest to our car but the farthest from the bank. A sign indicated that this ATM was set up for wireless service; I am not registered for that kind of service with Nedbank, so I used my ATM card instead. I inserted the card, received the money, quickly put the money into my pants pocket, and then removed the ATM card from the machine. The machine did not, however, return to its standard state. Instead, a message continued flashing asking for my cell phone number.

At this moment the man next to me leaned over, looked at the screen, and said, "Be careful, the machine is still on." He told me to reinsert my card and then press cancel. I was hesitant. Suddenly, three of the locals who were milling nearby converged on me with the same advice. One even reached around me and began punching numerous buttons on the machine. I was confused. Everyone was talking simultaneously, with half speaking in English and half speaking Tsonga. It was a stressful situation. I wanted to flee but was afraid to do so since it seemed that the machine was still on. Hence, others could withdraw money from my account.

Finally, the person who had been standing beside me at the other machine took control. He told everyone to be quiet. He turned toward me and in impeccable English said that he would clear everyone away from the ATM so that he and I could talk. He thus shooed away the other three young men. Each of them stepped back two meters. All during this time, the ATM continued to flash a sign saying that it needed my cell phone number. The man then said, again, that I had to insert my card and press cancel to remove that request. He repeated that if I didn't do that, others could take money from my account.

I couldn't decide what to do. So I made the decision to take his advice and reinserted the ATM card. The cell phone request disappeared, but the machine wanted my identification code. The "consultant" said that I needed to put in my identification code to clear the machine. That request made me uneasy since I now suspected these folks were working in tandem and had some way of seeing the keypad. So I entered an incorrect code, which locked my card in the machine. My thought was that I could return to the bank the next day and request the card from a bank representative.

Later that night, as I reviewed this incident in my mind, I came to the realization that one of these folks was probably connecting to that ATM through a cell phone. That connection caused the sign; since I had already completed my transaction, the machine thought another transaction was in the process of beginning. But my "consultant" and friends convinced me that mine had not ended—even though it had.

As soon as I returned to the car, I called Alabama Credit Union and asked to have the card permanently locked. The credit union representative did so and added that the credit union's system had already perceived the problem and shut down the card. Interestingly, through online monitoring as well as a series of later calls to the credit union, I learned that there were fifteen attempted transactions on my card after it was cancelled. All fifteen were at the same location, and each occurred after I had left the scene.

One other incident occurred as I left the ATM. The three assistants who had converged on me earlier did so again. This time they wanted a "tip" for their assistance. The requests were aggressive. Earlier, each had been referring to me as "Friend." Now, one of them tried to stop me from walking away by addressing me as, "Hey, White Man." That is not a moniker that I am accustomed to hearing. I will answer to "Hey, Professor." And, of course, I am more than willing to be known as Old Man with Big Stick. But "Hey, White Man"? No way. I took offense. So I turned, stuck out my chest like the hairiest of baboons, and shouted "NO!" I then proceeded to waddle aggressively back toward the car. The men followed me briefly but turned and departed when they saw Fabulous waiting nearby. I gave Fabulous a two-hundred-rand tip.

I hope you folks are well.

Love,
Dad, the Almost Victimized Baboon

Needless to say, it had been a day of bouncing back and forth. In one direction, the experience with Rivers, Elsie, and Johannes made us feel like a part of an African family—until I was told to leave. Then, in another direction, the elephants returned, but not in the passive way we expected. Finally, the adventure at the ATM reminded us that not everyone in South Africa is our friend. Some may see you as an "easy mark." So while humility and respect are important, one must exercise caution in day-to-day living.

The Ping-Pong match continued the next morning in the Sabie Park television room. The internet connection in Sabie Park had been recently upgraded, so I decided to check emails there rather than driving to the Protea. Plus, at the time, I still was not certain if the elephants had ever left Sabie Park. So I did not want to go too far from Sally and the bush house.

Dear Dan and Laura,

Earlier this morning I was using the internet in the Sabie Park television room when Eva, the woman who operates the Sabie Park laundry room, came to visit. She had seen my car and wanted to talk.

Eva is probably in her early or mid-fifties. She has four children, three boys and a girl. One of the boys, Confidence, has finished college and is looking for full-time employment in an agricultural field. Cassandra, the girl, had just left for her first year of college a week earlier. We brought a reconditioned laptop for Cassandra to take to school. Eva and Cassandra very much appreciated the unsolicited gift.

After exchanging a few pleasantries, Eva asked if I was the person the Protea staff calls "The Professor." I smiled and said, "Yes." She then explained that she lives close to people who work at the Protea. One of these people is Johannes. Apparently, according to Eva, the locals had a discussion about my appearance at the services for Johannes's daughter. Some wondered who I was, others thought that my presence at the service was inappropriate, but Johannes, who apparently was involved in the conversation, cut off the discussion by saying that the visit meant very much to him.

Eva then continued with a strange but interesting question: "Do you know that the staff at the Protea care about you and your wife very much?" I told her that I suspected they did. Then, I quickly added that I hoped they knew that we care about them too. She smiled and said, "They do." Eva then repeated what she had said earlier—that the visit meant a lot to Johannes. I didn't know how to respond, so I smiled and said, "That's nice." I wish I had thought of a better response, but that was the best I could come up with on the spot.

I hope you folks are well.

Love,
Dad, the Tongue-Tied

It was still early in the day, but I could already feel that the Ping-Pong match was back in session.

CHAPTER TWENTY

Shock and Awe

As you grow up, always tell the truth, do no harm to others, and don't think you are the most important being on earth.
—Harper Lee

Sabie Park management sent crews to repair the damaged fence the day after the elephants broke it. But that evening the elephants broke through the fence again. The process repeated itself for three nights in a row. The herd would break the fence after dark, enter Sabie Park, mill around during the night, and then leave as soon as it became light. The ditch to the side of our bush house provided the path for the elephants to enter and to leave. We heard the elephants when they were coming in during the evening, and on two occasions we watched them saunter past our bedroom window as they left at daybreak.

The challenge was not just that the elephants were breaking the fence every night; it was also that they were beginning to damage other areas within Sabie Park. Pipes were being broken, fences demolished, outside showers destroyed, and trees uprooted. Even a water feature at the park headquarters was ruined through the elephants' efforts. Behavior of this ilk could not be tolerated for long.

An additional challenge surfaced after the third night of elephant break-ins. On the two previous evenings, between twenty and twenty-four elephants entered the park in the evening and left at daybreak. But on this occasion, ten elephants chose to stay after daybreak. This situation was fraught with peril. In addition to the physical damage they could do during the day, the elephants were also a hazard to the people living in the area. It was only a matter of time before someone got badly hurt.

I learned of the problem early that morning while talking with the new park superintendent, Johan Lawson. Johan told me that he and Bennie, a long-time Sabie Park employee who served as assistant game manager, were going out to look for the elephants.

Dear Dan and Laura:

Just to let you know that I have a new field of expertise: elephant herding. So if any of my other positions fall on hard times, I know that I can make a living herding elephants. Okay, here's the full story.

The elephants broke in again last night. However, unlike previous times, part of the herd did not leave Sabie Park when morning light broke. The result was that Johan, Bennie, and two other members of the Sabie Park staff went looking for the elephants with the intention of driving them back into the Kruger. This was an opportunity I had no intention of missing. I begged Johan to let me go along. He said yes, so long as I was very careful. I promised to be so.

Within minutes, thereafter, I found myself trekking through large swaths of Sabie Park, searching for elephants. I quickly noticed that while I was searching for the elephants visually, Johan and Bennie were supplementing the search through smells and sounds. Senses are an important part of living in the bush. My bush hearing has improved remarkably over the years. I can hear animals in ways that I never expected to be able to. But I'm still a rank amateur compared with people like Johan and Bennie. I have on multiple occasions watched Bennie bend his ear toward the bush, listen to sounds I could not hear, and then tell me what animal is nearby. I never heard a thing. Additionally, I have seen Bennie sniff a scene and report, "There are baboons nearby." He can even identify zebras by smell. It's amazing. Even after twelve years, while my senses have improved remarkably, I am nowhere near where Bennie is. He functions at a much higher level. It is easy to be humble in the presence of a bush master.

We found the herd within fifteen minutes. The elephants were milling about some houses located in the central part of Sabie Park, approximately two kilometers from the Kruger. As Johan and Bennie were studying the herd and determining the best path in which to direct them, I asked a seemingly casual question about safety: "Have we brought along anything to protect us if the elephant's charge?" Instantly, Johan produced a slingshot from his back pocket. "This is all we need," he replied. The slingshot looked small. I should add, with admiration, that Johan never again removed the slingshot from his pocket.

After a few more minutes of study, Johan and Bennie selected the path they wanted the elephants to follow. They then began shouting, yelling, and clapping at the herd. Elephants respond to noise, I learned, but it is unwise, if not impossible, to intimidate an elephant by walking toward it. An elephant will often walk away if you walk toward it. But that departure is the elephant's choice—not an act of being intimidated. The entire team therefore stayed at least twenty meters away from the herd. Needless to say, they looked like small yapping dogs in comparison to the elephants.

Amazingly, the elephants began moving. Unfortunately, the herd moved toward the highway rather than the Kruger. This movement was problematic since there is, as previously mentioned, a fence between Sabie Park and the highway. The immediate fear was that the herd might break the fence and get outside the protection of both Sabie Park and the Kruger. So our team—notice how quickly I became part of the crew?—stopped making noise and repositioned itself at an angle between the fence and the herd.

The mention of "angle" here is important. We did not place ourselves directly between the fence and the herd. Johan's slingshot was not going to be too effective if the herd charged straight toward the fence and we were caught between them. So we stayed at an angle between the herd and fence.

The positioning—along with Johan and Bennie's resumed clapping and shouting—worked. The herd turned away from the highway fence and began moving toward the Kruger. We were definitely driving the elephants in a predetermined direction. A most impressive feat!

We successfully drove the herd to the Kruger fence but then encountered a second problem. The area to which we drove the herd was one where the Kruger fence was still standing. But, to our consternation, the herd refused to break the fence. The elephants seemed to want to "make a stand" at the fence rather than knock it down and return to the Kruger. It was ironic that the elephants, who had so willingly damaged and crossed the fence from Kruger into Sabie Park, were now unwilling to break the fence and return from Sabie Park into Kruger. Elephants? Who can know what they think?

Let me humbly confess that up to this point I was merely tagging along. I wasn't shouting, clapping, or doing anything to guide the elephants in any direction. I was a sponge trying to learn what I could. And I was striving to get to know Johan and Bennie better. As previously noted, both have more knowledge about the bush than any safari guide I have ever met. Both also love the bush. Bennie, for instance, shared while we were walking that he would just as soon remove the fence and allow the elephants to roam freely in Sabie Park. The majority of homeowners would never let this happen, of course, since it would result in landscape changes and possible damage to their homes—plus the danger of having the elephants constantly present. But the fact that he shared this information with me gave a fuller insight into Bennie and his love for the bush and its inhabitants.

Johan taught me that the key to driving a herd of elephants is to never make them angry. If a member of the herd got angry, Johan observed, then the entire herd could turn around and move toward us. That would be a problem that a slingshot couldn't solve.

Soon, however, I was able to serve a larger purpose within our herding team. I became a source of elephant knowledge. As it became obvious that the herd was unwilling to break through the fence to return to the Kruger, Johan turned and asked if I knew where the herd had entered the park. I did. It was in the ditch beside our house. I willingly shared that information with Johan.

"Then we must drive them back there," Johan observed. "These elephants are missing their leader and will only go out where the matriarch led them in."

So that's what we did. We shouted, clapped, and drove the elephants back toward the driveway of our bush house. It was just like the old Wild West, except we were moving elephants, not cows. Also, whereas the cows moved on the wide-open plains, the elephants crashed with reckless abandon over bushes, briars, and even small trees. Eventually, we got the elephants back to our driveway. They seemed to instantly recognize where they were and scooted through the fence in the area that had just been repaired. The elephants did not hesitate to break the fence beside our house.

In the end, Johan was standing beside the again-destroyed fence shouting, "Get out of here, and don't come back." I should add, though, that by this point Johan's shouting seemed mostly for show. Johan's and Bennie's care, concern, and respect for the elephants was readily apparent. Both are true lovers of the bush and its inhabitants

I hope you folks are well.

Love,
Dad, the Herder of Elephants

My participation in this herding operation provided additional evidence that my relationship with the elephants was changing. Rather than sitting together, I was imposing my will on them. Our Elephant had already left Sabie Park for the day; she was not in the group that I was herding. However, having learned how effectively elephants communicate with one another, I was certain she would learn of my involvement in this activity.

Events the following evening provided further evidence that Our Elephant recognized the change in our relationship. The herd broke through the fence at 21:30. Previously, the elephants had tended to move quickly past our house and disperse throughout Sabie Park. This time four elephants remained close to the house. One of them was Our Elephant. We watched as best we could in the dark; however, the evening was cloudy with little ambient light. We flashed our torch, when possible, to see what the elephants were doing. We knew we had to be careful, so we did not move far from the house.

Mostly the elephants milled about, breaking branches and eating leaves. When we went to sleep at 23:00, the foursome was still nearby.

Around 1:00 Sally heard a noise and woke me up. It was the sound of an elephant rubbing against our house.

I grabbed a torch and snuck outside. I peeked around the corner and found Our Elephant rubbing her hindquarters against the outside wall of the house. This wall separates our bedroom from the bush. She was leaning against it and scratching. I clapped my hands and shouted at her to stop doing that. She did. Then she ambled off into the bush.

This rubbing activity was extremely dangerous. The elephant could knock down the walls of the house with very little effort. Additionally, if she turned and began ramming the house with her head—an action elephants do to knock over trees—then I'm certain she would have collapsed not just the wall but the entire house.

The elephant forays into Sabie Park continued for four more nights. None of the elephants tried to push on our house during these visits. But Sabie Park residents continued to report broken fences, toppled trees, and damaged pipes. Even though I took a sort of perverse joy in hearing about the elephants' exploits in Sabie Park, I knew the situation was becoming untenable. Lots of people were complaining to Johan and Bennie.

The morning after the fourth night of destruction I awoke and discovered Johan, Bennie, and Peter, my friend who had helped me get the baboon removed from the tree, standing beside the mangled fence in our backyard. I joined them and learned they were exploring ways to stop the elephants from coming into Sabie Park. The concern extended beyond the physical damage the elephants were doing; they were worried about someone getting hurt. A collision of some sort seemed inevitable.

The team mentioned three alternatives, each of which had pros and cons. The first involved increasing the electrical power going to the fence. The fence was being rebuilt daily, but the staff was unable to find time to get the fence electrified before it was torn down again at night. This first approach would involve an "all-hands-on-deck" effort to reconstruct and electrify the fence in a single day. The fence had not been "hot" since it was destroyed more than two weeks ago. The idea, again, was not just to electrify the fence but to maximize the power as well. The shock had to be so painful that the elephants would not come back. The danger in this approach was that someone, especially a child, could accidentally touch the fence and suffer severe consequences.

One advantage of this approach was that it was not permanent. Once the elephants learned not to touch the fence, the power could be reduced. A second advantage was that we were, at that moment, the only family in Sabie Park living near the fence. So all we had to do was avoid touching the fence. I even asked, a bit naïvely, if the elephants could be hurt (i.e., killed) by the increased power. The team said that they didn't think so. That was obviously not the intent.

The second solution involved placing beehives in the area. Elephants hate honeybees and will go out of their way to avoid them. Beehive fences are constructed to keep elephants away from areas in which farmers grow crops. The hives are located ten meters apart and are constructed on flexible wires. Thus, if the elephants hit the wires, the hives swing and bees descend from numerous locations to harass the elephants.

The challenge to the bee solution is that it is permanent. Once the bees establish a presence in the area, they remain. This presents a two-fold problem: First, some residents might be allergic to bee stings. Hence the solution might even be more dangerous than the problem. Second, once bees become present in an area, they make residing in the area extremely uncomfortable. At least three of Kruger's camps, Skukuza, Satara, and Lower Sabie, have serious bee problems. People eating in the area are constantly bothered by bees, including having them go into drink cans, land on food, and be a general nuisance.

The final solution was to relocate part of the herd. Although it wasn't mentioned specifically, the implied idea was to move the matriarch and one or two other elephants further into the Kruger. Moving the entire herd would be too expensive. The underlying premise was that the matriarch was the one leading the herd across the fence each night. If she were removed, then the intrusions would stop.

The problem with this alternative was that we know elephants are relational. This herd is the matriarch's family. If we removed her from her family, we were condemning her to a life of loneliness and depression. Arguably, she might even die from the trauma. Plus, we know that elephants study and learn from one another. Thus, the next matriarch—the one "in waiting"—obviously knew how to break the fence and get into Sabie Park. So no matter where we moved the matriarch, the herd's next leader would know what to do. Repatriation would, thus, not solve the problem.

The team left to mull over these alternatives. I returned to the back stoep to ponder what I had done. I realized that while Our Elephant had crossed the fence physically, I had crossed it symbolically. While I had thought that I was just sitting with the elephants the previous summer, I had actually gone far beyond that. I had bonded with them. I, too, had "crossed the line." By doing so, I had created a situation in which all of the solutions were unsavory. Each alternative was going to disadvantage one or more members of the herd. It even occurred to me that perhaps I was the one who should move, although that alternative was not one that I preferred either.

After a variety of consultations, the Sabie Park team decided to try the shock treatment. A Sabie Park staff member stopped by the house in midafternoon to inform us of the decision. We were told that the fence would be electrified within an hour and warned to stay away. The power was obviously going to be very high. I asked about the consequences of touching the fence and was assured that it would not be life-threatening. However, there was no guarantee that I would remain conscious. Those observations were enough for me. I stayed away from the fence.

That evening we decided to have a braai.

Dear Dan and Laura,

Mom and I decided to have a braai this evening. We had not done so since the break-ins began because we were not certain about the safety of being outside in the dark while elephants tramped about. The fence is now fully electrified, so we felt safe giving a braai a try.

Initially, all was well. The weather was beautiful, the moon was bright, and there was not a cloud in the sky. Then, about 20:00, we heard elephants in the Kruger. I flashed my torch into the Kruger but couldn't see the elephants. We could, however, hear the breaking of branches. A full herd was obviously in the area.

At 20:20 the quiet of the night was interrupted. The first sound was soft: the wire of the fence rattled. The second sound was loud: it combined loud trumpeting with screams of pain. If that was Our Elephant, she had obviously received a "shocking" surprise. Mom cringed at the noise. Agony was in the air.

The elephant hit the fence thirty meters to the side of our boma. After the trumpeting stopped, she walked along the fence toward us. A quick check with our torches revealed that it was Our Elephant. She was obviously upset.

She stopped walking when she got beside the boma. At this point she paused and emitted an extremely loud grumbling noise from her stomach. Stomach noises are one of the many ways that elephants communicate. This message was being sent either to other elephants or to me. If to other elephants, then the grumbling meant, "Be careful. Those people have really increased the voltage of the fence." If the message was to me, then it was, "You bastard. That hurt!" In any case, after she communicated her message, she turned and walked back into the bush.

Mom was upset as well. We talked briefly, and I defended the shock treatment as being best both for the elephant's safety as well as that of the people who live in Sabie Park. Mom understood the argument but contended that there had to have been a gentler way to solve the problem. We talked for a few more minutes, then Mom stood up, picked up her water glass, and walked into the house. The evening was obviously over.

Before Mom went into the house, she turned and asked a question I treated as rhetorical: "Why did Our Elephant have to suffer just because you wanted to sit with her?" Fortunately, I didn't have to answer the question to which I had no response, having already identified it as rhetorical.

I hope you folks are well.

Lonesome Dad

We remained in Sabie Park a little more than a week after this incident. Our Elephant never returned. Nor did any other elephants. Unlike the previous year, we were alone when we took down the lanterns, pulled in the chairs from the back stoep, and locked the doors for the year. Our visit was over.

My colleague Lonnie Strickland and I talked frequently about the experience with Our Elephant after we had both returned to Alabama for another academic year. Lonnie suggested that the term "habituation" might provide a softer, less negative description of what happened between Our Elephant and me. From a psychological perspective, habituation refers to the way an organism ceases to respond to stimuli after repeated presentations. Ring a bell beside a cat long enough, and the cat will stop responding to the sound. From a wild animal's perspective, habituation refers to the way that an animal can become accustomed to the presence of humans. Appear with enough frequency in front of a wild animal, and that animal will stop being afraid or will at least become less cautious in your presence. Metaphorically, the fence between the animal and the person disappears.

In many ways, Our Elephant became habituated to us and we to her. Events proved that this condition was in neither of our best interests. I was almost trampled by a herd of trotting elephants, Our

Elephant suffered a severe shock for crossing the fence, and our bush house was almost pushed over by Our Elephant. Each of these events could have had devastating outcomes.

The tendency to endow elephants and other wild animals with human characteristics is a corollary to habituation. It is another way of crossing the fence; only in this instance we metaphorically pull the animal across to our side and contend that she must be like us. Anthropomorphizing these animals undercuts the validity of their existence as creatures of the wild. Domesticated animals should remain domesticated. One doesn't turn a pet dog loose in the African bush. Perhaps, in most instances, the wild should remain wild as well. We don't need to pull them across the fence and attribute human characteristics to them.

In fact, it might be wise to invert our perspectives. Let's keep the fence between us by studying animals on their own and see if we can simultaneously gain insights into our own behavior. Thus, instead of trying to understand animals by identifying characteristics similar to ours, we should begin to look at ourselves and identify ways we are similar to wild animals. We should not say, "Elephants mourn their dead as we do." Instead, we should say, "We mourn our dead as elephants do." That change in perspective is important. The center of attention does not always have to be us. This change in perspective can be illuminating.

Consider, for instance, the way young male elephants leave the herd. Somewhere in mid-adolescence, males are pushed out of the herd by the matriarch and other senior elephants. This separation occurs when adolescent males begin causing problems within the herd. These problems range from fighting to wanton destruction of the environment. The adolescent elephants thus get forced from the herd for bad behavior and go out into the bush and wander about on their own or in small groups for a couple of years. Eventually, if the male elephants are fortunate, they are permitted to join another herd. But their admission includes having to take behavior lessons from a senior elephant in the new herd. This senior elephant instructs the young elephants on what is and is not acceptable behavior in the herd. The senior elephant chastises and corrects inappropriate behavior and determines if and when the young elephant will be admitted into this new group.

A drive down the main street of most cities shows young men

wandering about in a manner quite similar to these adolescent elephants. On corners we see young men removed from one herd and struggling to find "herds" to which they belong. And sometimes we see similar wanton, needless destruction. But whereas senior elephants willingly take on the task of educating these elephants and helping them become productive members of another herd, we tend to allow our young to aimlessly wander and drift from place to place with little or no mentorship. They get advice not from senior leaders but from other adolescents who are in similar or perhaps even worse conditions. Couldn't we learn from the elephants? Couldn't we develop more ways for our senior elephants to advise and guide our lost youth? Are we guiding and mentoring our young as well as we should? All in all, the elephant approach seems far superior to what we do at present.

The analogies could go on, but the point is clear. It is arrogant to study animals to identify their human characteristics. Instead, we need to study and learn about characteristics that the animals have and import some of their wisdom into our own behaviors. To think our approach is best is the epitome of arrogance. If the elephants teach us anything, it is the importance of humility.

People with whom I have shared these elephant experiences say that the story needs an upbeat ending. Many observe that the tale cannot end with the elephant being shocked and our flying back to the United States. Others suggest we need a more optimistic ending.

These suggestions are probably true, but we must also be honest. This is not a work of fiction. But from the optimistic side, it is a pleasure to report that the Our Elephant returned two years after getting the shock. She milled about the area and recognized us sitting on the back stoep. She has continued to return occasionally since then, but she always remains far from the fence.

Last year Our Elephant returned and even brought along part of her family—three young elephants. She paraded the youngsters past us from afar.

She brought the youngsters with her on three additional visits. Each time she stayed thirty to forty meters away from the fence.

Eventually I began to wonder if she wanted to be closer—a final, inappropriately arrogant thought, I must confess. So on her third visit with the children, I walked toward the fence to get closer.

It was a mistake to do so. Our Elephant flattened her ears against her head, lifted and curled in her trunk, trumpeted, and rigorously charged toward me. I retreated rapidly. It was readily apparent to me that this was not a mock charge. After I retreated she seemed content. She casually ambled back toward her family.

The meaning of this final charge remains a puzzle. One interpretation might be that she wanted to retain a professional distance. Like me, she discovered the necessity of keeping a fence between us. The other interpretation might be that she was trying to protect me from the fence. The moment I backed safely away from the fence she stopped charging. Perhaps she did not want me to have to suffer the same fate she did. Only Our Elephant knows the true meaning of that charge. It is a mystery to which I have no need to know the answer.

CHAPTER TWENTY ONE

The Beautiful Mysteries

I see *mystery* not as something you *cannot* understand; rather it is something that you can *endlessly understand*! There is no point at which you can say, "I've got it." Always and forever, mystery gets you!
—Richard Rohr, Richard Rohr's Daily Meditations: The Center for Action and Contemplation

Aristotle observed that we can never achieve happiness by seeking it directly. If we want to be happy, do something else—ideally, something good for someone else. Then, if we are fortunate, we might inadvertently stumble into finding ourselves happy.

A similar observation can be made about humility. The best path for achieving humility comes not from trying to be humble but from being less selfish, less self-promoting, and a little less arrogant. Do the job, take care of the nitty-gritty details of life, and let our work and accomplishments speak for themselves. If we behave in this manner, others will take notice; this recognition is more positive and sincere than any posting on Facebook or LinkedIn. Ironically, by following this path, we will also find that fulfillment, satisfaction, and humility sneak in on the side. Mysteriously, it works.

One of the early chapters of *Sitting with Elephants* mentions how difficult it is to transition from the highly connected modern world to the disconnected world of the African bush. While true, that observation is only half of the story. It is equally difficult to transition from South Africa back to the United States. Everything seems noisy, rushed, almost overwhelming upon our return. Algorithms and chat bots again become matters of concern, replacing leopards, lions, and hyenas. Yet both locations have a purpose. They are different, but neither is superior to the other. Humility teaches us to acknowledge the validity and importance of both locations. We must also remember that life in either location can be joyful, invigorating, and mysterious. It can even be fascinatingly curious. To return to the opening metaphor, we must not just "Squeeze the Juice"; we should also look at each and every drop and say, "Isn't that interesting?" And perhaps, just perhaps, we don't have to know the meaning or the cause of each drop. Oftentimes, we should just enjoy the squeeze.

As I reflect on the experiences shared in this book, I realize that my relationship with the elephant changed as I began to be more public about it. Please don't misunderstand that observation. There is nothing inherently wrong with being public about a relationship. It is healthy, at least so long as you are sharing information about the relationship and not promoting it.

But in my case, I crossed a barrier. Slowly, I left the sharing path and crept over to promotion. The crossing occurred when I publicly expressed the desire to travel beneath the fence and be touched by the elephant. At that point, I began working in my interest, not Our Elephant's. I was trying to have new experiences to mention in future presentations. If the experiences had occurred, I would probably have taken pictures and posted them on Instagram with the implied commentary of "look what I did."

While not evil, these motives were self-centered, selfish, and mildly arrogant. They might even provide an answer to the question Sally posed as to why Our Elephant had to suffer so that I could sit with her. The answer, which I state with embarrassment, is that I was being selfish. I was thinking of my experiences, not those of Our Elephant.

A mysterious, synchronistic connection between what happened with Our Elephant and the events described at the funeral for Johannes's daughter is also evident. Recall that Elsie wisely told me to leave after I had stayed an appropriate length of time at the service. If I had remained, as I arrogantly began wanting to do, I would have crossed the fence into a private world of grief. Only my African friends belonged there. If I had remained, I would have inadvertently but inevitably made social miscues in the service or in the events that surrounded the service. These miscues would have drawn attention to me and would have interrupted and perhaps undercut the grieving process that Johannes and others in his community needed to undergo. That would have been tragic. Elsie sensed this danger. She recognized my transport mission was accomplished. She thus wisely told me to leave. Elsie kept the fence between us.

Although a bit more painful, perhaps the shock that Our Elephant suffered sent a somewhat similar message to her. She needed an Elsie to send her away. Wild elephants and people cannot live together. We need a fence between us. If we remove it, then either the people have to move further away or the elephants have to be domesticated. Neither option is good. The reconstructed fence, along with the recognition that we need to stay some distance from one another, provide a good lesson for all of us.

One of the many benefits of my fascination with elephants has been the willingness of others to share their elephant stories with me. All I have to do is listen. Some of these stories may be apocryphal, but others, especially when you consider the sources, are verifiable. Often these stories remind us that elephants are mysterious animals that we are far from understanding. Two particular stories deserve a brief mention.

The first story comes from Graham Spence, the coauthor of *The Elephant Whisperer*, the best book ever written about elephants. I became electronic friends with Mr. Spence when he graciously agreed to read an early version of this book.

As our friendship grew, I felt empowered to ask Mr. Spence about an incident that I had heard repeatedly from fans of his book, but about which I was not certain was true. The story, the first part of which was verifiable, was that Lawrence Anthony, his coauthor and brother-in-law, and the person who had the amazing elephant encounters, had unfortunately passed away while on a trip to Central Africa. This unfortunate event occurred after *The Elephant Whisperer* was published.

The second part of the story, which was unconfirmed, was that before Lawrence Anthony's wife learned of his death, the herd of elephants with which he had bonded came to his house and exhibited mourning rituals. Mr. Spence confirmed that the story was true.

I have additionally heard that the elephants return each year and exhibit mourning behavior close to the time of Lawrence Anthony's death. Thus, in some mysterious way, these animals seem to understand time and remember affections. What mysterious, magnificent beings.

The second story, which was shared by our game manager, Johan, dealt with the herd with which I interacted. One year, after we left, the elephants broke through the fence to Sabie Park. No one knows exactly what happened next, but a young elephant was found dead in a neighboring yard. No visible signs indicated that another animal had killed the young elephant. Nor, to anyone's knowledge, had a human intervened. Sabie Park officials removed the young elephant's body and kept the skeleton at headquarters.

For each of the next two years, the herd broke through the fence during the week of the young elephant's death. On each occasion, the herd made its way to headquarters, stayed for one evening, and then returned to Kruger early the next morning.

To determine if the visits were related to the remains of the infant elephant, and to save the expense of having to repair the fence, Johan and the Sabie leadership moved the remains back into the Kruger. Amazingly, the fence-breaking stopped. Even more amazing, the herd still showed up at the appointed time, but now stayed close to where the remains had been deposited. Sometimes truth is stranger than fiction.

Each of these stories increases one's curiosity about elephants. While a scientist might justly explain these behaviors based on temperature, sunlight, or some other environmental phenomenon, I prefer to simply enjoy the mystery. Not everything has to be explained.

When I first started teaching at Alabama, I had the good fortune of becoming friends with Morris Mayer, a professor who was a local legend. Morris had many mantras for which he was known, as well as a few idiosyncrasies. However, anyone who became friends with Morris had the pleasure of hearing him repeatedly argue that academics and students had a privilege that had to be paid to society. Morris called it "Paying Your Civic Rent."

Through this line Morris meant that each of us has talents and opportunities that have been given to us without recompense. It is selfish to use these gifts only for our own advantage. We owe it to society and to humankind to offer back at least partial payment for the gifts and opportunities we have been provided. If we think of the planet as a gift, then we have an obligation to return the gift in a little better condition than we received it. "But," Morris always added with a twinkle in his eyes, "no matter how much you give back, life always has a way of paying you forward even more." It was a mystery that Morris accepted.

Many of us dream of someday having lots of money and sharing it with those in need. But if we are honest with ourselves, we must admit that we are just getting by and acknowledge that the odds are slim to none that we will ever accumulate enough wealth that our gift will make a difference in many people's lives. We must leave these game-changing donations to the Bill Gateses and Warren Buffetts of the world.

Yet this lack of resources doesn't mean that what we do is not important. It is vastly important. But that "doing" involves simple acts of kindness, expressions of concern, attendance at important events, or perhaps even a pat on the back when things are not going well. These acts, from a mysterious, symbolic perspective, might be as important to some people as curing malaria is to others.

Recently, I was teaching an MBA class in Singapore. I started the class by talking about our elephant experiences and stressed the importance of humility in all aspects of life, including business. Forty percent of the business students in the class were from Indonesia; each of the Indonesians was Muslim.

At the beginning of the third and final day of the class, at which point we were deeply into communication issues, one of the Indonesians raised his hand and asked if he could say something. I replied, "Certainly."

He then recited what I had previously said about elephants and humility. He also mentioned a few other concepts that had been brought up in class. Then he added that he was aware that I was from the United States and, with apologies, added that he didn't like many people from the United States. Too often, he asserted, Americans come to Indonesia to tell everyone how to do things better. These experts, he added, never inquire as to why Indonesians do things in certain ways. Instead, the Americans just presume their way is better and tell Indonesians how to do it. Humility, the student concluded, seemed a concept foreign to the United States.

I listened intently as he spoke. When he was finished, I was a bit flummoxed as to what to say. So I asked him how he wanted me to respond. His answer was most interesting. He said he didn't want me to respond; he just wanted to give me a hug. So we did—right in the middle of a classroom with fifty other people present. Class members applauded.

My Muslim student then told the class that he had never hugged anyone who had sat with a herd of elephants. I responded that I had never hugged anyone superficially. That statement elicited another hug from my newfound friend and additional applause from the class. Those hugs were more valuable to me than that student will ever know. He paid me forward without ever realizing he did.

Africa, the African bush, the people of Africa, and the animals that inhabit the environs have hugged our hearts. Each has provided our family with profound lessons about the beautiful complexities and mysteries of the world and our own insignificance within it.

Yet, despite our insignificance, Africa has taught us that what we do is important. Africa has taught us that we can bond and become friends with people on the other side of the planet. These people may hold varying views on matters of religion, spirit, or business. It makes no difference. They are our friends. And that friendship is mysteriously valuable.

Africa has taught us that we can share food, money, belongings, friendship, and love with others who are financially less fortunate than us. Their financial challenges provide opportunities for us to show that we care. And though comparatively small, these gifts do make a difference in individual lives—and they add value to our own lives.

Africa has taught us that we can nod appreciatively, smile warmly, and offer a sincere and respectful "thanks" to guards, waiters, and others who serve society in various capacities. These gestures take little effort and cost nothing. But they can gently touch another person's heart—and mysteriously soften our own as well.

Finally, Africa has taught us that we can experience one final, ultimate mystery. We can sit with elephants in our backyard. That is more than a mystery; it is a beautiful gift.

Afterword

And so we beat on, boats against the current,
borne back ceaselessly into the past.
—F. Scott Fitzgerald, *The Great Gatsby*

We should all be thankful for those people
who rekindle the inner spirit.
—Albert Schweitzer

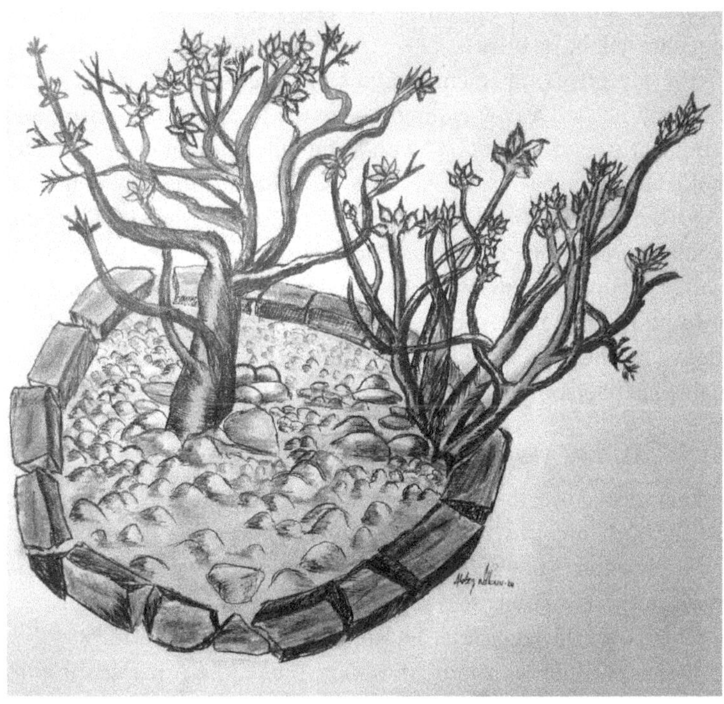

Twenty years ago I wrote a light-hearted business mystery entitled *Who Killed Keyboard?* The dramatic incident powering the book was that one character, Keyboard, had been killed during a power outage. The narrator, a computer mouse named Double Click, invites the reader to join the search for Keyboard's killer.

An early draft of the book left the identify of Keyboard's killer unresolved. In fact, the ending left much business unfinished. This intentional ambiguity seemed artistic.

I shared copies of the draft with local business executives and listened closely to their reviews. Unanimously the executives called the book cute, interesting, funny, and a good read. However, with even more unanimity, the executives bemoaned the ending. Stated simply, they said, "The ending sucks!" My defense of artistic ambiguity received boos, jeers, and catcalls.

Eventually, one executive took me aside and said, "Listen, if you want to write a successful business book, then you can't leave us 'hanging.' Business people don't like ambiguity. Even more importantly," he went on, "you have to resolve the situations in a positive way. Business people are inherently optimistic. We take risks because we think the outcome will be positive."

The executive's statement caused a light bulb to flash in my mind; the book needed a new ending. I scurried to my writer's garret and produced an ending that had wonderful outcomes for each character in the book. The change worked. The book did surprisingly well.

However, *Who Killed Keyboard?* was fiction; *Sitting with Elephants* is fact. The events in *Sitting with Elephants* actually happened. And in reality, life and time march on. Not everything works out as planned or to perfection. Yet like the executives, we must be hopeful and optimistic. So here, in synopsis, is what happened to some of the book's main characters.

Our Friends

Mike and Lynda Crosby, the couple who introduced us to living in the bush, divorced while *Sitting with Elephants* was in preparation for publication. Mike suffered a severe stroke a few months later and passed away. His family sent some of his ashes and asked us to distribute them over the fence into the Kruger. We did so prayerfully.

Our friendship with John and Mary Burke, the American friends who were visiting when the elephants first broke through the fence, continued throughout the years. John, unfortunately, developed Parkinson's and bravely battled it with Mary supporting him throughout. Eventually, Parkinson's won. John passed away peacefully in September of 2023, with Mary faithfully by his side.

Lonnie Strickland, the friend and university colleague who introduced us to South Africa and who, along with Mike Crosby, identified that a house was present before we made the internet purchase, is healthy, resilient, and doing well. He retired from the University of Alabama in May of 2023 after serving on the faculty for fifty-five years. More than forty years ago, Lonnie and I began "Squeezing the Juice" by completing a marathon together. Our current plan is to keep "squeezing" by climbing Mount Kilimanjaro.

The Hotel and the Staff at the Protea and Sabie Park

Proving that nothing is permanent, Marriott sold the Protea to a private investor group in 2022. The hotel is now called The Kruger Gate Hotel. The hotel has undergone a thorough renovation, relocating much of the food service and even removing the television room where the safari guides congregated.

Within the Protea staff, here is what I know: Calvin, the server who promised to bring food to our house when we got old, passed away from COVID. Elsie, the server who informed us about the passing of Johannes's daughter and who later told me to leave the funeral, retired during COVID and passed away from undetermined causes the next year. I learned of both of their passings when I returned to South Africa after COVID restrictions were lifted. Tears welled up in my eyes when I learned that these friends were gone.

Johannes, the man who lost his daughter in a car accident, continues to work at the hotel. So does Mbkaphi, the server known as Hidden. Mbkaphi's limp has become worse, and he struggles to get up and down steps. That impediment undercuts his job effectiveness. It's hopeful to see that the hotel has kept him on staff. It's even more hopeful to observe how other younger servers go out of their way to assist Mbkaphi. There is obvious respect, perhaps even love, for his tenacity. He sets an example for all to emulate.

Johan, the Sabie park manager, and Bennie, his assistant—both of whom invited me on the hunt to remove the herd of elephants after they broke through the fence—have both left Sabie Park. Johan found a new spiritual direction and works as a missionary in a Zambian orphanage. He sends pictures of himself playing soccer with local children. He looks contented. Bennie retired from Sabie Park and moved to the Highveld to be closer to family.

Our Elephant

The matriarchal elephant with whom I bonded has not returned to our backyard during any of my subsequent visits. COVID closed down the border in 2020, so I'm not sure if she came back that year. I have watched for her constantly in subsequent years but have not seen an elephant with her ear markings or her personality.

My Sally

Sally passed away from kidney failure on January 6, 2023. She had been ill for a number of years. Her last visit to South Africa in the summer of 2019 was strenuous. The flight over took a toll on her body, and the drive from Johannesburg to Sabie Park took double the time it normally takes because she was in such pain. By this point in life, she needed assistance to get out of a wheelchair.

Once we got to the bush house, Sally spent most of her time in the bedroom. She made it to the main room on a few special occasions. She was never able to go into Kruger Park or even drive around Sabie Park.

I have reflected often on Sally's visits to Africa. The more I think about them, the more I am amazed at the tenacity she showed from the beginning until the end. While it didn't seem relevant at the time of writing the book, it now seems important to mention that Sally had cerebral palsy and had a difficult time with mobility, especially as she aged. She also had ulcerative colitis, which led to her having an ostomy. So for all of the time we were exploring South Africa, Sally was dealing with mobility challenges as well as having to worry about a colostomy bag. Perhaps in addition to stressing the need for humility, this book should have stressed the need to appreciate the challenges other's face.

Sally spent the first seven months of COVID—from March 2020 until October 2020—in a rehabilitation facility after having been hospitalized with kidney problems. When I brought her home, she was barely able to get out of bed. Through it all, however, she always talked lovingly of Africa and of our friends there. She took great joy in listening to the audio version of this book, which she did multiple times. Even more importantly, she always talked optimistically about wanting to get well enough to make one more trip to the house. The thought of returning to Africa invigorated her mind even as her body declined. Together we lived with the harmless untruth that one more visit would happen.

Dan's family, Laura's family, and I carried her remains to Sabie Park in July of 2023. On the way I had vague ideas as to where to distribute her ashes. Perhaps on the road where we once saw a leopard. Or near a camp called Satara, where we once watched a pride of lions. Or near Skukuza, where an elephant once chased us. But as soon as we arrived, I knew where the ashes should go. Two impala lilies that we had planted beside the house years ago were struggling to survive. The African bush had overtaken them, and I had not had time to clear off the site during my brief visits after 2019. Dan's family and I spent a day cleaning and preparing the site. Then, when Laura's family arrived, we read Bible verses and scattered the ashes between the two impala lilies. One day I plan to join her there.

A few days later, after Dan's and Laura's families left to return to the United States, I walked out to look at the site on what would have been our fiftieth wedding anniversary. The impala lilies were in full bloom and seemed reinvigorated by the removal of the smothering bush as well as their newfound purpose. Up to this point, I had continued to wear my wedding ring. When friends asked if I was ever going to remove it, I replied, "I'll know when." Standing there, looking at the impala lilies shining in the bright sunlight, I knew it was time. I removed my wedding ring and placed it on a branch that overhangs where Sally's remains are distributed. It will watch over her until I return. My hope is that the ring will grow into the branch. It's an affirming symbol of what we had.

On occasion people ask if I intend to sell the African bush house. Others inquire about whether I'm going to keep going back to South Africa without Sally. Recent visits have led to the decision to return for as long as I am able. Importantly, these visits provide a final lesson about elephant wisdom. Stated simply, the stories about elephants continuing to return to special places, especially to sites where other elephants have died, now carry new significance. Revisiting an important location provides a way to keep alive cherished memories shared with those we loved. The visits provide peace, meaning, and a reaffirmation of life. The visits are even energizing, in that they simultaneously connect the past, the present, and the future. We savor memories of joyful and formative times with loved ones; we even extract wisdom and meaningful lessons from which to grow. We Squeeze the Juice and reflect on each moment available to us in the present. And, finally, we amble forward slowly, like elephants, toward a future that we optimistically believe has meadows we can forage and challenges we can overcome. It's a good way to live.